THE PHILOSOPHY OF ART

THE PHILOSOPHY OF ART

H. TAINE

TRANSLATOR: JOHN DURAND

Denton & White
2016

The Philosophy of Art – this particular edition – was originally published in 1873.

PUBLISHERS' NOTE.

The now famous name of Taine was first introduced to the American public by the issue, in 1865, of a small imported edition of this work. That edition has long been out of print here and in Europe. That the book is now reissued may be subject of special satisfaction to those who already possess the Author's "*Ideal in Art*" "*Art in the Netherlands*" and "*Art in Greece*" as this work (now published in a style uniform with others named) is properly the forerunner of them all; containing, as it does, the principles laid down in the Author's first course of lectures, and constantly referred to in the later courses which now form the books before alluded to.

In preparing this edition for the press, the translator, by bringing to bear the experience gained in the later works, has made it a great improvement on the previous edition.

PREFACE TO THE FIRST EDITION.

The translation herewith presented to the reader consists of a course of Lectures delivered during the winter of 1864, before the Students of Art of the *École des Beaux Arts* at Paris, by H. Taine, *Professeur d'Esthétique et d' Histoire de l'Art* in that institution.

These lectures, as a system of Æsthetics, consist of an application of the experimental method to art, in the same manner as it is applied to the sciences. Whatever utility the system possesses is due to this principle. The author undertakes to explain art by social influences and other causes; humanity at different times and places, climate, and other conditions, furnish the facts on which the theory rests. The artistic development of any age or people is made intelligible through a series of historical inductions terminating in a few inferential laws, constituting what the title of the book declares it to be—*the philosophy of art.*

Such a system seems to possess many advantages. Among others, it tends to emancipate the student of art, as well as the amateur, from metaphysical and visionary theories growing out of false theories and traditional misconceptions; he is not misled by an exclusive adherence to particular schools, masters, or epochs. It also tends to render criticism less capricious, and therefore less injurious; dictating no conventional standard of judgment, it promotes a spirit of charity towards all works. As there is no attempt to do more than explain art according to natural laws, the reader must judge whether, like all systems assuming to bring order out of confusion, this one fulfils its mission.

Readers familiar with M. Taine's able and original work on English literature *(Histoire de la Littérature Anglaise)* will recognize in the following pages the same theory applied to art as is therein applied to literature.

LONDON, *November 9,* 1865.

PREFACE TO THE SECOND EDITION.

Since the publication of the first edition of the "*Philosophy of Art*" seven years ago, in London, its author has become deservedly popular, and especially in this country. His writings are sought for, read and translated both in England and on the continent of Europe, and it would be but refining gold to say aught in his praise. Like every man of genius he has, as time moves on, improved in his order of thought and in his wonderfully artistic style. His latest work, "*On Intelligence*" ranks him as high among thinkers, as his former works among men of letters.

The present edition is a careful revision of the former one, and amounts, indeed, to a new translation. Were either to be compared with the original, no change of sense could probably be detected. The present edition, however, being much more literal, the translator considers it an improvement, and hopes that it will be found more worthy of its gifted author, the publishers, his indulgent critics, and the public generally.

SOUTH ORANGE, N. J. *January,* 1873.

CONTENTS.

Objects and method of Æsthetics—
Opposition of the Historic and Dogmatic
Methods—Laws—Sympathy for all Schools—
The Analogy between Æsthetics and Botany,
and between the Natural and the Moral Sci-
ences.

§ II.

What is the Object of Art—The Research Experimental and not Ideal—Comparisons and
Eliminations of Works of Art sufficient.

Division of the Arts into two groups—On the
one hand, Painting, Sculpture and Poesy; and,
on the other, Architecture and Music. First
group—Imitation apparently the end of Art—
Reasons for this derived from ordinary experi-
ence, and from the lives of great men; Michael
Angelo, Corneille—Reasons derived from the
History of Art and Literature; Pompeii and
Ravenna—Classic Style under Louis XIV., and
Academic Style under Louis XV.

§ III.

Exact Imitation not the end of Art—
Illustrations derived from Casting, Photog-

raphy, and Stenography—Comparison between Denner and Van Dyck—Certain Arts purposely Inexact—Comparison between Antique Statues and Draped Figures in the Churches of Naples and Spain—Comparison between Prose and Verse—The Two Iphigenias of Goethe

§ IV.

Relationships of Parts the true object of Imitation—Illustrations derived from Drawing and Literature.

§ V.

A Work of Art not confined to Imitating Relationships of Parts—Modification of the Principle in the greatest Schools; Michael Angelo, Rubens—The Medici Tomb—The 'Kermesse.'

Definition of Essential Character: Examples of the Lion and the Netherlands.

Importance of Essential Character; Nature imperfectly expressing it, Art supplies her place—Flanders in the time of Rubens, and Italy in the time of Raphael.

Artistic Imagination—Spontaneous Impressions, and their power of Transformation.

Retrospect; successive steps of the Method, and Definition of a Work of Art.

§ VI.

Two Parts in this Definition—How Music and Architecture enter into it—Opposition of the first and second group of Arts—The first copies Organic and Moral Dependencies; the second combines Mathematical Dependencies.

Mathematical Relationships perceived by the sense of sight—Different classes of these Relationships—Principle of Architecture.

Mathematical Relationships perceived by the sense of Hearing—Different classes of these Relationships—Principle of Music—The second Principle of Music, Analogy of the Sound and the Cry—Music, on this side, enters into the first group of Arts.

The definition given is applicable to all the Arts.

§ VII.

The Value of Art in Human Life—Selfish Acts for the preservation of the Individual—Social Acts tending to preserve the Species—Disinterested Acts having for object the contemplation of Causes and Essentials—Two ways for attaining this end; Science and Art—Advantages of Art.

PART II.

PRODUCTION OF THE WORK OF ART.

§ I.

General Law for the Production of the Work of Art—First Formula—Two sorts of Proof, one of Experience, and the other of Reasoning.

§ II.

General Exposition of the Action of Social Mediums—The Development of the Plant compared with the Development of Human Activity—Natural Selection.

§ III.

The Action of a Moral Temperature—The Influence of Melancholy and Cheerful States of

Mind—The Artist is saddened by his personal share of misfortune—By the melancholy ideas of his contemporaries—By his aptitude for defining the salient character of objects, which here is sadness—He finds suggestions and enlightenment only in melancholy subjects—The Public comprehends only melancholy subjects.

An inverse case, state of prosperity and general joy—Intermediate cases.

§ IV.

Real and Historical cases—Four Epochs, and four leading Arts.

§ V.

Greek Civilization and Antique Sculpture—Comparison of Greek manners with those of contemporaries—The City—The Citizen—Taste for War—The Athlete-Spartan Education—The Gymnasium in other parts of Greece.

Conformity of Customs with Ideas—Nudity—Olympic Games—The Gods perfect Human Figures.

Birth of Sculpture; Statues of Athletes and of Gods—Why Statuary sufficed for the Artist's Conceptions—Immense Number of Statues.

§ VI.

The Civilization of the Middle Ages, and Gothic Architecture.

Decline of Antique Society—Invasions of Barbarians—Feudal Excesses—Universal Misery.

Distaste for Life—Exalted Sensibility—The Passion of Love—Power of the Christian Religion.

Birth of Gothic Architecture—The Cathedral—Universality of Gothic Architecture.

§ VII.

French Civilization in the Seventeenth Century, and Classic Tragedy.

The Courtier—Ruling Taste—Tragedy—The Aristocratic Sentiments of Society— Importation of French Tragedy into other European Countries.

§ VIII.

Contemporary Civilization and Music—The French Revolution—Effect of Civil Equality, Machinery, and the Comforts of Existence—Decay of Traditional Authority.

The Representative Man—Development of Music—Its Origin in Germany and Italy; and its Dependence on Modern Sentiments.

Universality of Music.

§ IX.

The Law of the Production of Works of Art—The Four Terms of the Series—Practical Application of the Law to a Study of all the Arts and of every Literature.

§ X.

Application of the Law to the Present—The Social Medium renewing itself constantly, Art renews itself—Hopes for the Future.

ON THE NATURE OF THE WORK OF ART.

GENTLEMEN:

In commencing this course of lectures I wish to ask you two things of which I stand in great need: in the first place, your attention; afterwards, and especially, your kind indulgence. The warmth of your reception persuades me that you will favor me with both. Let me sincerely and earnestly thank you beforehand. The subject with which I intend to entertain you this year is the history of art, and, principally, the history of painting in Italy. Before entering on the subject itself, I desire to indicate to you its spirit and method.

I.

The principal point of this method consists in recognizing that a work of art is not isolated, and, consequently, that it is necessary to study the conditions out of which it proceeds and by which it is explained.

The first step is not difficult. At first, and evidently, a work of art—a picture, a tragedy, a statue—belongs to a certain whole, that is to say, to the entire work of the artist producing it. This is elementary. It is well known that the different works of an artist bear a family likeness, like the children of one parent; that is to say, they bear a certain resemblance to each other. We know that every artist has his own style, a style recognized in all his productions. If he is a painter, he has his own coloring, rich or impoverished; his favorite types, noble or ignoble; his attitudes, his mode of composition, even his processes of execution; his favorite pigments, tints, models, and manner of working. If he is a writer, he has his own characters, calm or passionate; his own plots, simple or complex; his own dénouements, comic or tragic, his peculiarities of style, his pet periods, and even his special vocabulary. This is so true, that a connoisseur, if you place before him a work not signed by any prominent master, is able to recognize, to almost a certainty, to what artist this work belongs, and, if sufficiently experienced and delicate in his perceptions, the period of the artist's life, and the particular stage of his development.

This is the first whole to which we must refer a work of art. And here is the second. The artist himself, considered in connection with his productions, is not isolated; he also belongs to a whole, one greater than himself, comprising the school or family of artists of the time and country to which he belongs. For example, around Shakespeare, who, at the first glance, seems to be a marvellous celestial gift coming like an aerolite from heaven, we find several dramatists of a high order—Webster, Ford, Massinger, Marlowe, Ben Jonson, Beaumont and Fletcher—all of whom wrote in the same style and in the same spirit as he did. There are the same characters in their dramas as in Shakespeare's, the same violent and terrible characters, the same murderous and unforeseen occurrences, the same sudden and frenzied passions, the same irregular, capricious, turgid, magnificent style, the same exquisite poetic feeling for rural life and landscape, and the same delicate, tender, affectionate ideals of woman.

In a similar way Rubens is to be judged. Rubens apparently stands alone, without either predecessor or successor. On going to Belgium, however, and visiting the churches of Ghent, Brussels, Bruges, or Antwerp, you find a group of painters with genius resembling his. First, there is Crayer, in his day considered a rival; Seghers, Van Oost, Everdingen, Van Thulden, Quellin, Hondthorst, and others, with whom you are familiar, Jordaens, Van Dyck—all conceiving painting in the same spirit, and with many distinctive features, all preserving a family likeness. Like Rubens, these artists delighted in painting ruddy and healthy flesh, the rich and quivering palpitation of life, the fresh and sensuous pulp which is diffused so richly over the surface of the living being, the real, and often brutal types, the transport and abandonment of unfettered action, the splendid lustrous and embroidered draperies, the varying hues of silk and purple, and the display of shifting and waving folds. At the present day they seem to be obscured by the glory of their great contemporary; but it is not the less true that to comprehend him it is necessary to study him amidst this cluster of brilliants of which he is the brightest gem— this family of artists, of which he is the most illustrious representative.

This being the second step, there now remains the third. This family of artists is itself comprehended in another whole more vast, which is the world surrounding it, and whose taste is similar. The social and intellectual condition is the same for the public as for artists; they are not isolated men; it is their voice alone that we hear at this moment, through the space of centuries, but, beneath this living voice which comes vibrating to us, we distinguish a murmur, and, as it were, a vast, low sound, the great infinite and varied voice of the people, chanting in unison with them. They have been great through this harmony, and it is very necessary that it should ever be so. Phidias and Ictinus, the constructors of the Parthenon and of the Olympian Jupiter, were, like other Athenians, pagans and free citizens, brought up in the *palæstra,* exercising and wrestling naked, and accustomed to deliberate and vote in the public assemblies; possessing the same habits, the same interests, the same ideas, the same faith; men of the same race, the same education, the same language; so that in all the important acts of their life they are found in harmony with their spectators.

This harmony becomes still more apparent if we consider an age nearer our own. For example, take the great Spanish epoch of the sixteenth and a part of the seventeenth centuries, in which lived the great painters, Velasquez, Murillo, Zurbaran, Francisco de Herrera, Alonzo Cano, and Morales; and the great poets, Lope de Vega, Calderon, Cervantes, Tirso de Molina, Don Luis de Leon, Guilhem de Castro, and so many others. You know that at this time Spain was entirely monarchical and Catholic; that she had over-come the Turks at Lepanto; that she planted her foot in Africa and maintained herself there; that she combated the Protestants in Germany, pursued them in France and attacked them in England; that she subdued and converted the idolaters of the new world, and chased away Jews and Moors from her own soil; that she purged her own faith with autodafés and persecutions: that she lavished fleets and armies, and the gold and silver of her American possessions, along with her most precious children, the vital blood of her own heart, upon multiplied and boundless crusades, so obstinately and so fanatically, that at the end of a century and a half she fell pros-

trate at the feet of Europe, but with such enthusiasm, such a burst of glory, such national
fervor, that her subjects, enamored of the
monarchy in which their power was concentrated, and with the cause to which they devoted their lives, felt no other desire than that
of elevating religion and royalty by their obe-
dience, and of forming around the Church and
the Throne a choir of faithful, militant, and
adoring supporters. In this monarchy of cru-
saders and inquisitors, preserving the chivalric
sentiments and sombre passions, the ferocity,
intolerance, and mysticism of the middle ages,
the greatest artists are the very men who possessed in the highest degree the faculties, sentiments, and passions of the public that surrounded them. The most celebrated poets—
Lope de Vega and Calderon—were military
adventurers, volunteers in the Armada, duellists and lovers, as exalted and as mystic in
love as the poets and Don Quixotes of feudal
times; they were passionate Catholics and so
ardent that, at the end of their lives, one became a familiar of the Inquisition, others became priests, and the most illustrious among
them—the great Lope de Vega—fainted on

saying Mass, at the thought of the sacrifice and martyrdom of Jesus. Everywhere may be found similar examples of the alliance, the intimate harmony existing between an artist and his contemporaries; and we may rest assured that if we desire to comprehend the taste or the genius of an artist, the reasons leading him to choose a particular style of painting or drama, to prefer this or that character or coloring, and to represent particular sentiments, we must seek for them in the social and intellectual conditions of the community in the midst of which he lived.

We have therefore to lay down this rule: that, in order to comprehend a work of art, an artist or a group of artists, we must clearly comprehend the general social and intellectual condition of the times to which they belong. Herein is to be found the final explanation; herein resides the primitive cause determining all that follows it. This truth, gentlemen, is confirmed by experience. In short, if we pass in review the principal epochs of the history of art, we find that the arts appear and disappear along with certain accompanying social and intellectual conditions. For example, the Greek tragedy—that of Æschylus, Sophocles, and Euripides—appears at the time when the Greeks were victorious over the Persians; at the heroic era of small republican cities, at the moment of the great struggle by which they acquired their independence and established their ascendency in the civilized world; and we see it disappearing along with this independence and this vigor when a degeneracy of character and the Macedonian conquest delivered Greece over to strangers. It is the same with Gothic architecture, developing along with the definitive establishment of feudalism in the semi-renaissance of the eleventh century at the period when society, delivered from brigands and Normans, began to consolidate, and disappearing at the period when the military system of petty independent barons, with the manners and customs growing out of it vanished near the end of the fifteenth century, on the advent of modern monarchies. It is the same with Dutch painting, which flourished at the glorious period when, through firmness and courage, Holland succeeded in freeing herself from Spanish rule, combated England with equal power, and became the richest, freest, most industrious, and most prosperous state in Europe: and we see it declining at the commencement of the eighteenth century, when Holland, fallen into a secondary rank, leaves the first to England, reducing itself to a well-ordered, safely administered, quiet, commercial banking-house, in which man, an honest *bourgeois,* could live at ease, exempt from every great ambition and every grand emotion. It is the same, finally, with French tragedy appearing at the period when a noble and well-regulated monarchy, under Louis XIV., established the empire of decorum, the life of the court, "the pomp and circumstance" of society, and the elegant domestic phases of aristocracy; disappearing when the social rule of nobles and the manners of the antechamber were abolished by the Revolution.

I would like to make you more sensible by a comparison of this effect of the social and intellectual state on the Fine Arts. Suppose you are leaving the land of the south for that of the north; you perceive on entering a certain zone a particular mode of cultivation and a particular species of plant: first come the aloe and the orange; a little later, the vine and the olive; after these, the oak and the chestnut; a little further on, oats and the pine, and finally, mosses and lichens. Each zone has its own mode of cultivation and peculiar vegetation; both begin at the commencement, and both finish at the end of the zone; both are attached to it. The zone is the condition of their existence; by its presence or its absence is determined what shall appear and what shall disappear. Now, what is this zone but a certain temperature; in other words, a certain degree of heat and moisture; in short, a certain number of governing circumstances analogous in its germ to that which we called a moment ago the social and intellectual state?

Just as there is a physical temperature, which by its variations determines the appearance of this or that species of plant, so is there a moral temperature, which by its variations determines the appearance of this or that species of art. And as we study the physical temperature in order to comprehend the advent of this or that species of plants, whether maize or oats, the orange or the pine, so is it necessary to study the moral temperature in order to comprehend the advent of various phases of art, whether pagan sculpture or realistic painting, mystic architecture or classic literature, voluptuous music or ideal poetry. The productions of the human mind, like those of animated nature, can only be explained by their *milieu*.

Hence the study I intend to offer you this season, of the history of painting in Italy. I shall attempt to lay before your eyes the mystic *milieu,* in which appeared Giotto and Beato Angelico, and to this end I shall read passages from the poets and legendary writers, containing the ideas entertained by the men of those days concerning happiness, misery, love, faith, paradise, hell, and all the great interests of humanity. We shall find documentary evidence in the poetry of Dante, of Guido Cavalcanti, of the Franciscans, in the Golden Legend, in the Imitation of Jesus Christ, in the Fioretti of St. Francis, in the works of historians like Dino Campagni, and in that vast collection of chroniclers by Muratori, which so naively portray the jealousies and disturbances of the small Italian republics. After this I shall attempt to place before you in the same manner the pagan *milieu* which a century and a half later produced Leonardo da Vinci, Michael Angelo, Raphael and Titian, and to this end I shall read, either from the memoirs of contemporaries—Benvenuto Cellini for instance—or from the diverse chronicles kept daily in Rome and in the principal Italian cities, or from the despatches of ambassadors, or, finally, from the descriptions of fêtes, masquerades, and civic receptions, which are remarkable fragments, displaying the brutality, sensuality, and vigor of society, as well as the lively poetic sentiment, the love of the picturesque, the great literary sentiment, the decorative instincts, and the passion for external splendor which at that time are seen as well among the people and the ignorant crowd as among the great and the lettered.

Suppose now, gentlemen, we should succeed in this undertaking, and that we should be able to mark clearly and precisely the various intellectual conditions which have led to the birth of Italian painting—its development, its bloom, its varieties and decline. Suppose the same undertaking successful with other countries, and other ages, and with the different branches of art, architecture, sculpture, painting, poetry, and music. Suppose, that through the effect of all these discoveries, we succeed in defining the nature, and in marking the conditions of existence of each art, we shall then have a complete explanation of the Fine Arts, and of all in general; that is to say, a philosophy of the Fine Arts—what is called an *æsthetic* system. This is what we aim at, gentlemen, and nothing else. Ours is modern, and differs from the ancient, inasmuch as it is historic, and not dogmatic; that is to say, it imposes no precepts, but ascertains and verifies laws. Ancient Æsthetics gave, at first, a definition of beauty, and declared, for instance, that the beautiful is the expression of the moral ideal, or rather is the expression of the invisible, or, rather still, is the expression of the human passions; then starting hence, as from an article of a code, they absolved, condemned, admonished, and directed. It is my good fortune not to have such a formidable task to meet. I do not wish to guide you—it would embarrass me too much. Besides, I say with all humility, that, as to precepts, we have as yet found but two: the first is to be born a genius, an affair of your parents, and not mine; and the second, which implies much labor in

order to master art, which likewise does net
depend on me, but on yourselves. My sole duty is to offer you facts, and show you how
these facts are produced. The modern method,
which I strive to pursue, and which is beginning to be introduced in all the moral sciences,
consists in considering human productions,
and particularly works of art, as facts and productions of which it is essential to mark the
characteristics and seek the causes, and nothing more. Thus understood, science neither
pardons nor proscribes; it verifies and explains. It does not say to you, despise Dutch
art because it is vulgar, and prize only Italian
art; nor does it say to you despise Gothic art
because it is morbid, and prize only Greek art.
It leaves every one free to follow their own
predilections, to prefer that which is germane
to one's temperament, and to study with the
greatest care that which best corresponds to
the development of one's own mind. Science
has sympathies for all the forms of art, and for
all schools, even for those the most opposed
to each other. It accepts them as so many
manifestations of the human mind, judging
that the more numerous they are, and the

more antithetical, the more they show the human mind in its innumerable and novel phases. It is analogous to botany, which studies the orange, the laurel, the pine, and the birch, with equal interest; it is itself a species of botany, applied not to plants, but to the works of man. By virtue of this it keeps pace with the general movement of the day, which now affiliates the moral sciences with the natural sciences, and which, giving to the first the principles, precautions, and directions of the second, gives to them the same stability, and assures them the same progress.

II.

I wish to apply at once this method to the first and principal question by which a course of æsthetics is opened out, and which is a definition of art. What is art, and in what does its nature consist? Instead of establishing a formula, I wish to familiarize you with facts, for facts exist here as elsewhere—positive facts open to observation; I mean *works* of *art* arranged by families in galleries and libraries, like plants in an herbarium, and animals in a museum. Analysis may be applied to the one as to the others; a work of art may be investigated generally, as we investigate a plant or an animal generally. There is no more need of discarding experience in the first case than in the second; the entire process consists in discovering, by numerous comparisons and progressive eliminations, traits common to all works of art, and, at the same time, the distinctive traits by which works of art are separated from other productions of the human intellect.

To this end we will, among the five great arts of poetry, sculpture, painting, architecture, and music, set aside the last two, of which the explanation is more difficult, and to which we will return afterwards; we shall at present consider only the three first. All, as you are aware, possess a common character, that of being more or less *imitative* arts.

At the first glance, it seems that this is their principal character, and their object is imitation as exact as possible. For it is plain that a statue is meant to imitate accurately a really living man; that a picture is intended to portray real persons in real attitudes, the interior of a house and a landscape, such as nature presents. It is no less evident that a drama, a romance, attempts to represent faithfully characters, actions, and actual speech, and to give as precise and as accurate a picture of them as is possible. When, accordingly, the image is inadequate or inexact, we say to the sculptor, "This breast or this limb is not well executed;" and to the painter, "The figures of your background are too large—the coloring of your trees is faulty;" and we say to the author, "Never did man feel or think as you have imagined him."

But there are other proofs, still stronger, and first, every-day experience. When we behold what takes place in the life of an artist, we perceive that it is generally divided into two sections. During the first, in the youth and maturity of his talent, he sees things as they are, and studies them minutely and earnestly; he fixes his eyes on them; he labors and worries to express them, and he expresses them with more than scrupulous fidelity. Arriving at a certain moment of life, he thinks he understands them thoroughly and discovers no more novelty in them; he casts aside the living model, and with certain prescribed rules which he has picked up in the course of his experience he forms a drama or a romance, a picture or a statue. The first epoch is that of natural feeling; the second that of mannerism and decline. If we penetrate the lives of the greatest men, we rarely fail to discover both. In the life of Michael Angelo, the first period lasted a long time, a little less than sixty years; all the works belonging to it disclose the sentiment of force and heroic grandeur. The artist is imbued with it; he has no other thought. His numerous dissections, his countless drawings, the unremitted analysis of his own heart, his study of the tragic passions and of their physical expression, are for him but the means of manifesting outwardly the militant energy with which he is carried away. This idea descends upon you from every corner of the great vault of the Sistine chapel. Enter the Pauline chapel alongside of it, and contemplate the works of his old age—the Conversion of St. Paul, the Crucifixion of St. Peter; consider even the Last Judgment, which he painted in his seventy-seventh year. Connoisseurs, and those who are not, recognize at once that the two frescoes are executed according to prescribed rules; that the artist possessed a certain number of forms, which he used conventionally; that he multiplied extraordinary attitudes, and ingeniously contrived foreshortenings; that the lively invention, naturalness, the great transport of the heart, the perfect truth peculiar to his first works, have, at least in part, disappeared from the abuse of technique and the force of routine; and that if he is still superior to others, he is greatly inferior to himself.

The same comment may be made on another life—that of our French Michael Angelo, Corneille. In the first years of his life, Corneille was likewise struck by the feeling of force, and of moral heroism. He found it around him in the vigorous passions bequeathed by the religious wars to the new monarchy; in the daring acts of duellists; in the proud feeling of honor which still carried away the devotees of feudalism; in the bloody tragedies which the plots of princes and the executions of Richelieu furnished as spectacles for the court; and he created personages like *Chimène* and the *Old.* like *Polyeucte* and *Pauline,* like *Cornélie, Sertorius, Émilie,* and *les Horaces.* Afterwards he produced *Pertharite, Attila,* and other feeble works, in which the situations merge into the horrible, and generous emotions lose themselves in extravagance. In this period the living models he once contemplated no longer had a social setting; at least he no longer sought them, he failed to renew his inspiration. He was governed by prescribed rules due to the memory of processes which he had formerly found in the heat of enthusiasm, literary theories, dissertations and distinctions on theatrical catastrophes and dramatic licenses. He copied and exaggerated himself; learning, calculation and routine shut out from him the direct and personal contemplation of powerful emotions and of noble actions; he no longer created, but manufactured.

It is not alone the history of this or that great man which proves to us the necessity of imitating the living model, and of keeping the eye fixed on nature, but rather the history of every great school of art. Every school (I believe without exception) degenerates and falls, simply through its neglect of exact imitation, and its abandonment of the living model. You see it in painting, in the fabricators of muscles and exaggerated attitudes who succeeded Michael Angelo; in the sciolists of theatrical decorations and in the brawny rotundities which have followed the great Venetians; and in the boudoir and alcove painters which closed the French school of art of the eighteenth century. The same thing occurs in literature, with the versifiers and rhetoricians of the Latin decadence; with the sensual and declamatory playwrights closing the bright period of the English drama, and with the manufacturers of sonnets, puns, witticisms, and bombast of the Italian decline. Among these I will cite two striking examples. The first is the decline of sculpture and painting in antiquity, of which you obtain a vivid impression by visiting Pompeii, and afterwards Ravenna. At Pompeii the painting and sculpture belong to the first century of the present era; at Ravenna the mosaics are of the sixth century, about the times of the Emperor Justinian. In this interval of five centuries art becomes irremediably corrupt, and its degeneracy is wholly due to the neglect of the living model. In the first century the pagan manners and tastes of the *palestra* still existed. Men wore their vestments loose and cast them off easily, frequented the baths, exercised in a state of nudity, witnessed the combats of the circus, ever contemplating sympathetically and intelligently the active movements of the living body. Their sculptors and painters, surrounded by nude and half-nude forms, were capable of reproducing them. Accordingly, you will see on the walls of Pompeii, in the little oratories and in the inner courts, beautiful dancing females, spirited, supple young heroes, with manly chests, agile feet, every posture and form of the body rendered with an ease and accuracy to which the most elaborate study of the present day cannot attain. During the following five hundred years everything gradually changes. Pagan manners, the use of the *palestra,* and the love of the nude, disappear. The body is no longer exposed, but concealed under complicated drapery, and under a display of lace, purple, and oriental magnificence. People no longer esteem the wrestler and the youthful gymnast,[1] but the eunuch, the scribe, the monk, and the woman. Asceticism gains ground, and with it a love for listless reverie, hollow disputation, scribbling and wrangling. The worn-out babblers of the Lower Empire replace the valiant Greek athletes and the hardy combatants of

Rome. By degrees the knowledge and study of the living model are interdicted. People have discarded it. Their eyes rest only on the works of ancient masters, and they copy these. Soon copies are only made of copies, and again copies of these, so that each generation recedes a step from the original type. The artist ceases to have his own idea and his own feeling, and becomes a copying machine. The Fathers declare that he must invent nothing, but must adhere to lineaments prescribed by tradition and sanctioned by authority. This separation of the artist from the living model brings art to the condition in which you see it at Ravenna. At the end of five centuries, artists can only represent man in two ways—seated and standing; other attitudes are too difficult, and are beyond their capacity. Hands and feet appear rigid as if fractured, the folds of drapery are wooden, figures seem to be mannikins, and heads are invaded by the eyes. Art is like an invalid sinking under a mortal consumption; it is languishing, and about to expire.

In a different branch of art amongst ourselves, and in a neighboring century, we find again a similar decline, and brought about by similar causes. In the age of Louis XIV., literature attained to a perfect style, to a purity, to a precision, to a sobriety of which we have no example; dramatic art, especially, created a language and a style of versification deemed by all Europe a masterpiece of the human intellect. This is due to the fact of writers finding their models around them and constantly observing them. The language of Louis XIV. was perfect, displaying a dignity, eloquence, and gravity truly royal. We know by the letters, despatches, and memoirs of the court personages of that time, that an aristocratic tone, sustained elegance, propriety of terms, dignified manners, and the art of correct speaking, were as common to courtiers as to monarch; so that the writer frequenting their society, had but to draw on his memory and experience in order to obtain the very best materials of his art.

[1] ἔφηβος.

III.

Is this true in every particular, and must we conclude that absolutely exact imitation is the end of art?

If this were so, gentlemen, absolutely exact imitation would produce the finest works. But, in fact, it is not so. In sculpture, for instance, casting is the process by which a faithful and minute impression of a model is obtained, and certainly a good cast is not equal to a good statue. Again, and in another domain, photography is the art which completely reproduces with lines and tints on a flat surface, without possible mistake, the forms and modelling of the object imitated. Photography is undoubtedly a useful auxiliary to painting, and is sometimes tastefully employed by cultivated and intelligent men; but after all, no one thinks of comparing it with painting. And finally, as a last illustration, if it were true that exact imitation is the supreme aim of art, let me ask what would be the best tragedy? the best comedy? the best drama? A stenographic report of a criminal trial, every word of which is faithfully recorded. It is clear, however, that if we sometimes encounter in it flashes of nature and occasional outbursts of sentiment, these are but veins of pure metal in a mass of worthless dross; it may furnish a writer with materials for his art, but it does not constitute a work of art.

Some may possibly say, that photography, casting, and stenography are mechanical processes, and that we ought to leave mechanism out of the question, and accordingly limit our comparisons to man's work. Let us, therefore, select works by artists conspicuous for minute fidelity. There is a canvas in the Louvre by Denner. This artist worked microscopically, taking four years to finish a portrait. Nothing in his heads is overlooked—the finest lines and wrinkles, the faintly mottled surface of the cheeks, the black specks scattered over the nose, the bluish flush of imperceptible veins meandering under the skin, nor the reflection of objects in the vicinity on the eye. We are struck with astonishment. This head is a perfect illusion; it seems to project out of the frame. Such success and such patience are unparalleled. Substantially, however, a broad sketch by Van Dyck is a hundredfold more powerful. Beside, neither in painting nor in any other art are prizes awarded to deceptions.

A second and stronger proof, that exact imitation is not the end of art, is to be found in this fact, that certain arts are purposely inexact. There is sculpture, for instance. A statue is generally of one color, either of bronze or of marble; and again, the eyes are without eyeballs. It is just this uniformity of tint, and this modification of moral expression, which completes its beauty. Examine corresponding works, in which imitation is pushed to extremity. The churches of Naples and Spain contain draped statues, colored; saints in actual monastic garb, with yellow earthy skins, suitable to ascetics, and bleeding hands and wounded sides characteristic of the martyred. Alongside of these appear madonnas, in royal robes, in festive dresses, and in bright silks, crowned with diadems, wearing precious necklaces, brilliant ribbons, and magnificent laces, and with rosy complexions, glittering eyes, and eyeballs formed of carbuncles. By this excess of literal imitation, the artist gives no pleasure, but repugnance, often disgust, and sometimes horror.

It is the same in literature. The best half of dramatic poetry, every, classic Greek and French drama, and the greater part of Spanish and English dramas, far from literally copying ordinary conversation, intentionally modify human speech. Each of these dramatic poets makes his characters speak in verse, casting their dialogue in rhythm, and often in rhyme. Is this modification prejudicial to the work? Ear from it. One of the great works of the age, the "Iphigenia" of Goethe, which was at first written in prose and afterwards re-written in verse, affords abundant evidence of this. It is beautiful in prose, but in verse what a difference! The modification of ordinary language, in the introduction of rhythm and metre, evidently gives to this work its incomparable accent, that calm sublimity, that broad, sustained tragic tone, which elevates the spirit above the low level of common life, and brings before the eye the heroes of ancient days—that lost race of primitive souls—and, among them, the august virgin, interpreter of the gods, custodian of the laws, and the benefactress of mankind, in whom is concentrated whatever is noble and good in human nature, in order to glorify our species and renew the inspiration of our hearts.

IV.

It is essential, then, to closely imitate something in an object; but not everything. We have now to discover what imitation should be applied to. Anticipating an answer to this, I reply, "To the relationships and mutual dependence of parts." Excuse this abstract definition—I will make my meaning clearer to you.

Imagine yourselves before a living model, man or woman, with a pencil, and a piece of paper twice the dimensions of your hand, on which to copy it. Certainly, you cannot be expected to reproduce the magnitude of the limbs, for your paper is too small; nor can you be expected to reproduce their color, for you have only black and white to work with. What you have to do is to reproduce their *relationships*, and first the proportions, that is to say, the relationships of magnitude. If the head is of a certain length, the body must be so many times longer than the head, the arm of a length equally dependent on that, and the leg the same; and so on with the other members. Again, you are required to reproduce forms, or the relationships of position: this or that curve, oval, angle, or sinuosity in the model must be repeated in the copy by a line of the same nature. In short, your object is to reproduce the aggregate of relationships, by which the parts are linked together, and nothing else; it is not the simple corporeal appearance that you have to give, but the *logic* of the whole body.

Suppose, in like manner, you are contemplating some actual character, some scene in real life, high or low, and you are asked to furnish, a description of it. To do this you have your eyes, your ears, your memory, and, perhaps, a pencil, to dot down five or six notes—no great means, but ample for your purpose. What is expected of you is, not to record every word and motion, all the actions of the personage, or of the fifteen or twenty persons that are figured before you, but, as before, to note proportions, connections, and relationships; you are expected, in the first place, to keep exactly the proportion of the actions of the personage, in other words, to give prominence to ambitious acts, if he is ambitious, to avaricious acts, if he is avaricious, and to violent acts, if he is violent; after this, to observe the reciprocal connection of these same acts; that is to say, to provoke one reply by another, to originate a resolution, a sentiment, an idea by an idea, a sentiment, a preceding resolution, and moreover by the actual condition of the personage; in addition to that, still by the general character bestowed on hi in. In short, in the literary effort, as in the pictorial effort, it is important to transcribe, not the visible outlines of persons and events, but the aggregate of their relationships and interdependencies, that is to say, their logic.

As a general rule, therefore, whatever interests us in a real personage, and which we entreat the artist to extract and render, is his outward or inward logic; in other terms, his structure, composition and action.

We have here, as you perceive, corrected the first definition given; it is not cancelled, but purified. We have discovered a more elevated character for art, which thus becomes intellectual, and not mechanical.

V.

Does this suffice us? Do we find works of art simply confined to a reproduction of the relationships of parts? By no means, for the greatest schools are justly those in which actual relationships are most modified. Consider, for example, the Italian school in its greatest artist, Michael Angelo, and, in order to give precision to our ideas, let us recall his principal work, the four marble statues surmounting the tomb of the Medicis at Florence. Those of you who have not seen the originals, are at least familiar with copies of them. In the figures of these men, and especially in the reclining females, sleeping or waking, the proportions of the parts are certainly not the same as in real personages. Similar figures exist nowhere, even in Italy. You will see there young, handsome, well-dressed men, peasants with bright eyes and a fierce expression, academy models with firm muscles and a proud bearing; but neither in a village nor at festivities, nor in the studios of Italy or elsewhere, at the present time or in the sixteenth century, does any real man or woman resemble the indignant heroes and the colossal despairing virgins which this great artist has placed before us in this funereal chapel. Michael Angelo found these types in his own genius and in his own heart. In order to create them it was necessary to have the soul of a recluse, of a meditative man, of a lover of justice; the soul of an impassioned and generous nature bewildered in the midst of enervated and corrupt beings, amidst treachery and oppression, before the inevitable triumph of tyranny and injustice, under the ruins of liberty and of nationality, himself threatened with death, feeling that if he lived it was only by favor, and perhaps only by a short respite, incapable of sycophancy and of submission, taking refuge entirely in that art by which, in the silence of servitude, his great heart and his great despair still spoke. He wrote on the pedestal of his sleeping statue—"Sleep is sweet, and yet more sweet is it to be of stone, while shame and misery last. Fortunate am I not to see— not to feel. Forbear to arouse me! Ah! speak low!"

This is the sentiment which revealed to him such forms. To express it, he has changed the ordinary proportions; he has lengthened the trunk and the limbs, twisted the torso upon the hips, hollowed out the sockets of the eyes, furrowed the forehead with wrinkles similar to the lion's frowning brow, raised mountains of muscles on the shoulder, ridged the spine with tendons, and so fastened the vertebras that it resembles the links of an iron chain strained to their utmost tension and about to break.

Let us consider, in like manner, the Flemish school; and in this school the great Fleming, Rubens, and one of the most striking of his works, the "Kermesse." In this work, no more than in those of Michael Angelo, will you find an imitation of ordinary proportions. Visit Flanders, and observe the types of mankind about you, even at feastings and revellings, such as the fêtes of Gayant, Antwerp, and other places. You will see comfortable-looking people eating much and drinking more; serenely smoking, cool, phlegmatic bodies; dull-looking, and with massive, irregular features, strongly resembling the figures of Teniers. As to the splendid brutes of the "Kermesse," you meet nothing like them! Rubens certainly found them elsewhere. After the horrible religious wars, this rich country of Flanders, so long devastated, finally attained peace and civil security. The soil is so good, and the people so prudent, comfort and prosperity returned almost at once. Everybody enjoyed this new prosperity and abundance; the contrast between the past and the present led to the indulgence of rude and carnal instincts let loose like horses and cattle after long privation in fresh, green fields, abounding in the richest pasture. Rubens himself was sensible of them; and the poetry of gross, sumptuous living, of satisfied and redundant flesh, of brutal, inordinate merry-making, found a ready outlet in the shameless sensualities and voluptuous ruddiness, in the whiteness and freshness of the nudities of which he was so prodigal. In order to express all this in the "Kermesse" he has expanded the trunk, enlarged the thighs, twisted the loins, deepened the redness of the cheeks, dishevelled the hair, kindled in the eyes a flame of savage, unbridled desire, unloosed the demons of disorder in the shape of shattered glasses, overturned tables, holdings and hissings, a perfect orgie, and the most extraordinary culmination of human bestiality ever portrayed upon canvas.

These two examples show you that the artist, in modifying the relationships of parts, modifies them understandingly, purposely, in such a way as to make apparent the *essential character* of the object, and consequently its leading idea according to his conception of it. This phrase, gentlemen, requires attention; this *essential character* is what philosophers call the *essence* of things; and because of this they say that it is the aim of art to manifest the *essence* of things. We will not retain this term essence, which is technical, but simply state that it is the aim of art to manifest a predominant character, some salient principal quality, some important point of view, some essential condition of being in the object.

We here approach the true definition of art, and accordingly need to be perfectly clear. We must insist on and precisely define essential character. I would premise at once that it is *a quality from which all others, or at least most other qualities, are derived according to definite affinities.* Grant me again this abstract definition: a few illustrations will make it plain to you.

The essential character of a lion, giving him his rank in the classifications of natural history, is that of a great flesh-eater; nearly all his traits, whether physical or moral, as I am about to prove to you, are derived from this trait as their fountain-head. First, there are physical traits: his teeth move like shears; he has a jaw constructed to tear and to crush; and necessarily, for, being carnivorous, he has to nourish himself with, and prey upon, living game; in order to manoeuvre this formidable instrument he requires enormous muscles, and for their insertion, temporal sockets of proportionate size. Add to the feet other instruments, the terrible contractile claws, the quick step on the extremity of the toes, a terrible elasticity of the thighs acting like a powerful spring, and eves that see best at night, because night is the best hunting-time. A naturalist, pointing to a lion's skeleton, once said to me, "There is a jaw mounted on four paws."

The moral points of the lion are likewise in harmony. At first, there is the sanguinary instinct—the craving for fresh flesh, and a repugnance for every other food; next, the strength and the nervous excitement through which the lion concentrates an enormous amount of force at the instant of attack and defence; and on the other hand, his somniferous habits, the grave, sombre inertia of moments of repose, and the long yawnings after the excitement of the chase. All these traits are derived from his carnivorous character, and on this account we call it his essential character.

Let us now consider a more difficult case, that of an entire country, with its innumerable details of structure, aspect, and cultivation; its plants, animals, inhabitants, and towns; as, for example, the Low Countries. The essential character of this region is its *alluvial* formation; that, is to say, a formation due to vast quantifies of earth brought down by streams and deposited about their mouths. From this single term spring an infinity of peculiarities, summing up the entire nature of the country, not only its physical outlines, what it is in itself, but again the intellectual, moral, and physical qualities of its inhabitants, and of their works. At first, in the inanimate world, come its moist and fertile plains, the necessary consequence of numerous broad rivers and vast deposits of productive soil. These plains are always green, because broad, tranquil, and sluggish streams, and the innumerable canals so easily constructed in soft, flat ground, maintain perennial verdure. You can readily imagine, and on purely rational principles, the aspect of such a country—a dull, rainy sky, constantly streaked with showers, and even on fine days veiled as if by gauze with light vapory clouds rising from the wet surface, forming a transparent dome, an airy tissue of delicate, snowy fleeces, over the broad verdant expanse stretching out of sight and rounded to the distant horizon. In the animated kingdom these numerous luxuriant pastures attract countless herds of cattle, who recline tranquilly on the grass, or ruminate over their cud, and dot the flat green sward with innumerable spots of white, yellow, and black. Hence the rich stores of milk and meat, which, added to the grains and vegetables raised on this prolific soil, furnish its inhabitants with cheap and abundant supplies of food. It might well be said that in this country water makes grass, grass makes cattle, cattle make cheese, butter, and meat; and all these, with beer, make the inhabitant. Indeed, out of this fat living, and out of this physical organization saturated with moisture, spring the phlegmatic temperament, the regular habits, the tranquil mind and nerves, the capacity to take life easily and prudently, unbroken contentment and love of well-being, and, consequently, the reign of cleanliness and the perfection of comfort. These consequences extend so far as even to affect the aspect of towns. In an alluvial country there is no stone; building material consists of terra-cotta bricks, and tiles. Rains being frequent and heavy, roofs are very sloping, and as dampness lasts a long time, their fronts are painted and varnished. A Flemish town, therefore, is a network of brown or red edifices always neat, occasionally glittering and with pointed gables; here and there rises an old church constructed of shingle or of rubble; streets in the best of order run between two scrupulously clean lines of sidewalk. In Holland the sidewalks are laid in brick, frequently intermingled with coarse porcelain: domestics may be seen at an early hour in the morning on their knees cleaning them off with cloths. Cast your eyes through the dazzling window-panes; enter a club-room decked with green branches, with its floor powdered with sand constantly renewed; visit the taverns, brightly painted, where rows of casks display their brown rotund pides, and where the rich yellow beer foams up out of glasses covered with quaint devices. In all these details of common life, in all these signs of inward contentment and enduring prosperity, you detect the effects of the great underlying characteristic which is stamped upon the climate and the soil, upon the vegetable kingdom and the animal kingdom, upon man and his works, upon society and the individual.

Through these innumerable effects, you judge of the importance of this essential character. It is this which art must bring forward into proper light, and if this task devolves upon art, it is because nature fails to accomplish it. In nature, this essential character is simply dominant; it is the aim of art to render it predominant. It moulds real objects, but it does not mould them completely: its action is restricted, impeded by the intervention of other causes; its impression on objects bearing its stamp is not sufficiently strong to be clearly visible. Man is sensible of this deficiency, and to remove it he has invented art.

Let us again take up Rubens' "Kermesse." These blooming merry wives, these roystering drunkards, these busts and visages of burly unbridled brutes, probably found counterparts in the carousals of the day. Over-nourished and exuberant nature aimed at producing such gross forms and such coarse manners, but she only half accomplished her task; other causes intervened to stay this excess of a carnal jovial energy. There is, at first, poverty. In the best of times, and in the best countries, many people have not enough to eat, and fasting, at least partial abstinence, misery, and bad air, all the accompaniments of indigence, diminish the development and boisterousness of native brutality. A suffering man is not so strong, and more sober. Religion, law, police regulations, and habits due to steady labor, operate in the same direction; education does its part. Out of a hundred subjects who, under favorable conditions, might have furnished Rubens with models, only five or six, perhaps, could be of any service to him. Suppose now that these five or six figures in the actual festivities which he might have seen were lost in a crowd of people more or less indifferent and common; consider again, that at the moment they came under his eye they exhibited neither the attitude, the expression, the gestures, the abandonment, the costume, or the disorder requisite to make this teeming excitement apparent. Through all these draw-backs nature called art to its aid; she could not clearly distinguish the character; it was necessary that the artist should supplement her.

Thus is it with every superior work of art. While Raphael was painting his "Galatea," he wrote that, beautiful women being scarce, he was following a conception of his own. This means that, looking at human nature from a certain point of view, its repose, its felicity, its gracious and dignified sweetness, he found no living model to express it satisfactorily. The peasant or laboring girl who posed for him, had hands deformed by work, feet spoiled by their covering, and eyes disordered by shame, or demoralized by her calling. His "Fornarina" has drooping shoulders, a meagre arm above the elbow, a hard and contracted expression.[1] If he painted her in the Farnesini Palace, he completely transformed her, developing a character in his painted figure of which the real figure only contributed parts and suggestions.

Thus the province of a work of art is to render the essential character, or, at least, some capital quality, the predominance of which must be made as perceptible as possible. In order to accomplish this the artist must suppress whatever conceals it, select whatever manifests it, correct every detail by which it is enfeebled, and recast those in which it is neutralized.

Let us no longer consider works but artists, that is to say, the way in which artists feel, invent, and produce: you will find it consistent with the foregoing conception of the work of art. There is one gift indispensable to all artists; no study, no degree of patience, supplies its place; if it is wanting in them they are nothing but copyists and mechanics. In confronting objects the artist must experience *original sensation*; the character of an object strikes him, and the effect of this sensation is a strong, peculiar impression. In other words, when a man is born with talent his perceptions—or at least a certain class of perceptions—are delicate and quick; he naturally seizes and distinguishes, with a sure and watchful tact, relationships and shades; at one time the plaintive or heroic sense in a sequence of sounds, at another the listlessness or stateliness of an attitude, and again the richness or sobriety of two complimentary or contiguous colors. Through this faculty he penetrates to the very heart of things, and seems to be more clear-sighted than other men. This sensation, moreover, so keen and so personal, is not inactive—by a counter-stroke the whole nervous and thinking machinery is affected by it. Man involuntarily expresses his emotions; the body makes signs, its attitude becomes mimetic; he is obliged to figure externally his conception of an object; the voice seeks imitative inflections, the tongue finds pictorial terms, unforeseen forms, a figurative, inventive, exaggerated style. Under the force of the original impulse the active brain recasts and transforms the object, now to illumine and ennoble it, now to distort and grotesquely pervert it; in the free sketch, as in the violent caricature, you readily detect, with poetic temperaments, the ascendency of involuntary impressions. Familiarize yourselves with the great artists and great authors of your century; study the sketches, designs, diaries, and correspondence of the old masters, and you will again everywhere find the same inward process. We may adorn it with beautiful names; we may call it genius or inspiration, which is right and proper; but if you wish to define it precisely you must always verify therein the vivid spontaneous sensation which groups together the train of accessory ideas, master, fashion, metamorphose and employ them in order to become manifest.

We have now arrived at a definition of a work of art Let us, for a moment, cast our eyes backward, and review the road we have passed over. We have, by degrees, arrived at a conception of art more and more elevated, and consequently more and more exact. At first we thought that the object of art was to *imitate sensible appearances*. Then separating material from intellectual imitation, we found that what it desired to reproduce in sensible appearances is the *relationships of paints*. Finally, remarking that relationships are, and ought to be, modified in order to obtain the highest results of art, we proved that if we study the relationships of parts it is *to maize predominant an essential character*. No one of these definitions destroys its antecedent, but each corrects and defines it. We are consequently able now to combine them, and by subordinating the inferior to the superior, thus to sum up the result of our labor:— "The end of a work of art is to manifest some essential or salient character, consequently some important idea, clearer and more completely than is attainable from real objects. Art accomplishes this end by employing a group of connected parts, the relationships of which it systematically modifies. In the three imitative arts of sculpture, painting, and poetry, these groups correspond to real objects."

[1] See the two portraits of the "Fornarina," in the Sciarra and the Borghese palaces.

VI.

That established, gentlemen, we see, on examining the different parts of this definition, that the first is essential and the second accessory. An aggregate of connected parts is necessary in all art which the artist may modify so as to portray character; but in every art it is not necessary that this aggregate should correspond with real objects; it is sufficient that it exists. If we therefore meet with aggregates of connected parts hich are not imitations of real objects, there will be arts which will not have imitation for their point of view. This is the case, and it is thus that architecture and music are born. In short, besides connections, proportions, moral and organic dependencies, which the three imitative arts copy, there are mathematical relationships which the two others, imitating nothing, combine.

Let us, at first, consider the mathematical relationships perceived by the sense of sight. Magnitudes sensible to the eye may form amongst each other aggregates of parts connected by mathematical laws. For instance, a piece of wood or stone may have geometrical form, that of a cube, a cone, a cylinder, or a sphere, which establishes regular relationships of distance between the different points of its outline. Furthermore, its dimensions may be quantities mutually related in simple proportions which the eye can seize readily; height, may be two, three, or four times greater than thickness or breadth: this constitutes a second series of mathematical relationships. Finally, many of these pieces of wood or stone may be placed symmetrically on the top or by the side of each other, according to distances and angles mathematically combined. Architecture is established on this aggregate of connected parts. An architect conceiving some dominant character, either serenity, simplicity, strength, or elegance, as formerly in Greece or Rome, or the strange, the varied, the infinite, the fantastic, as in Gothic times, may select and combine connections, proportions, dimensions, forms, and positions—in short, the relationships of materials, that is to say, certain visible magnitudes in such a way as to display the character aimed at.

By the side of magnitudes perceived by sight there are magnitudes perceived by the hearing,—I mean the velocities of sonorous vibrations; and these vibrations being magnitudes may also form aggregates of parts connected by mathematical laws. In the first place, as you are aware, a musical sound is composed of continuous vibrations of equal velocity, and this equality already places between them a mathematical relationship; in the second place, two sounds being given, the second may be composed of vibrations, two, three, or four times the rapidity of the first; accordingly, there is between these two sounds a mathematical relationship, which is figured by placing them at an equal distance from each other on the musical stave. If, consequently, instead of taking two, we take a number of sounds, and place them at equal distances,—we form a scale, which scale is the gamut, all the sounds being thus bound together according to their relative position on the gamut. You can now establish these connections either between successive or simultaneous sounds, the first order of sounds constituting melody, and the second harmony. This is music: it has two essential parts, based, like architecture, on mathematical relationships, which the artist is free to combine and modify.

Music, however, possesses a second property, and this new element gives it a peculiar quality and no ordinary scope. Besides its mathematical qualities, sound is analogous to the cry, and by this title it directly expresses with unrivalled precision, delicacy and force, suffering, joy, rage, indignation—all the agitations and emotions of an animated sensitive being, even to the most secret and most subtle gradations. From this point of view it is similar to poetic declamation, furnishing a specific type of music, called the music of expression, like that of Gluck and the Germans, in opposition to the music of melody, that of Rossini and the Italians. Let the composer's point of view be what it may, the two styles of music are nevertheless related to each other, sounds always forming aggregates of parts linked together at once by their mathematical relationship and by the correspondence which they have with the passions and the various internal states of the moral being. The musician, therefore, who conceives a certain salient, important feature of things, let it be sadness or joy, tender love or passionate rage, any idea or sentiment whatever, may freely select and combine in such a way in these mathematical and moral relationships as to manifest the character which he has conceived.

All the arts are thus included in the definition above presented. In architecture and music, as in sculpture, painting, and poetry, it is the object of a work of art to manifest some essential character, and to employ as means of expression an aggregate of connected parts, the relationship of which the artist combines and modifies.

VII.

Now that we know the nature of art, we can comprehend its importance. Previously we were only sensible of its effect; it was a matter of instinct, and not of reason: we were conscious of respecting and esteeming art, but were not qualified to account for our respect and esteem. Our admiration for art can now be justified, and we can mark its place in the order of life.

Man, in many respects, is an animal endeavoring to protect himself against nature and against other men. He is obliged to provide himself with food, clothing, and shelter, and to defend himself against climate, want, and disease. To do this he tills the ground, navigates the sea, and devotes himself to different industrial and commercial pursuits. Furthermore, he must perpetuate his species, and secure himself against the violence of his fellow-men; to this end, he forms families and states, and establishes magistracies, functionaries, constitutions, laws, and armies. After so many inventions and such labor, he is not yet emancipated from his original condition; he is still an animal, better fed and better protected than other animals; he still thinks only of himself, and of his kindred. At this moment a superior life dawns on him—that of contemplation, by which he is led to interest himself in the creative and permanent causes on which his own being and that of his fellows depend, in the leading and essential characters which rule each aggregate, and impress their marks on the minutest details. Two ways are open to him for this purpose. The first is Science, by which, analyzing these causes and these fundamental laws, he expresses them in abstract terms and precise formula; the second is Art, by which he manifests these causes and these fundamental laws no longer through arid definitions, inaccessible to the multitude, and only intelligible to a favored few, but in a sensible way, appealing not alone to reason, but also to the heart and senses of the humblest individual. Art has this peculiarity, that it is at once *noble* and *popular,* manifesting whatever is most exalted, and manifesting it to all.

PART II.

ON THE PRODUCTION OF THE WORK OF ART.

I.

Having investigated the nature of the work of art, there now remains a study of the law of its production. This law, in general terms, may be thus expressed:—*A work of art is determined by an aggregate which is the general state of the mind and surrounding circumstances.* I have stated this principle in the foregoing section, and have now to establish it.

This law rests on two kinds of proof: the one that of experience, and the other that of reason. The former consists of an enumeration of the many instances in which the law verifies itself. Some of these I have already presented to you, and others will soon follow. One may assert, moreover, that no case is known to which the law is not applicable; it is strictly so to those hitherto examined, and not merely in a general way, but in detail; not only to the growth and extinction of great schools, but again to all the variations and oscillations to which art is subject. The second order of proof consists in showing this dependence to be not only rigorous in point of fact, but, again, that it is so through necessity. We will accordingly analyze what we have called the general state of the mind and surrounding circumstances; we shall seek, according to the ordinary standard of human nature the effects which a like state must produce on the public, on artists, and consequently on works of art. Hence we draw a forced connection and a definite concordance, and we establish a necessary harmony which we had observed as simply fortuitous. The second proof *demonstrates* what the first had averred.

II.

In order to make this harmony apparent let us resume a comparison already of service to us, that between a plant and a work of art, and note the circumstances in which a plant, or a species of plant, say the orange, may be developed and propagated in a certain soil. Let us suppose all kinds of grain and seed borne by the wind and sown at random; on what conditions can those of the Lorange germinate, become trees, blossom, yield fruit, spread, and cover the ground with a numerous family?

Many favorable circumstances are essential to this end. And at first the soil must be neither too light nor too meagre: otherwise, the roots lacking depth and grasp, the tree would fall at the first gale of wind. Next, the soil must not be too dry; otherwise the tree will wither where it stands deprived of the moisture of springs and streams. Moreover, the climate must be warm; or the tree, which is delicate, will freeze, or at least droop, and never put forth sprouts; the summer must be long, in order that the fruit, which is slow in ripening, may fully mature; and the winter mild, so that January frosts may not blast or shrivel the oranges that remain green on its branches. Finally, the soil must not be too favorable for other plants, lest the tree, left to itself, might be stifled by the competition and infringement of a more vigorous vegetation. When all these conditions concur, the little orange will grow, become mature, and produce others again to reproduce themselves. Storms will undoubtedly occur, stones fall, and browsing goats will destroy certain plants; but on the whole, in spite of accidents which kill individuals, the species will be propagated, cover the ground, and in a few years display a nourishing grove of orange trees. All this is to be seen in the admirably sheltered gorges of Southern Italy, in the environs of Sorrento and Amain, on the shores of the gulfs, and in the small, watered valleys, freshened by streams descending from the mountains, and caressed by the beneficent breezes of the sea. This concourse of circumstances was necessary in order to produce those beautiful round tops, those lustrous domes of a bright deep green, those innumerable golden apples, and that exquisite fragrant vegetation which, in mid-winter, makes this coast the richest and loveliest of gardens.

Let us now reflect on the manner in which things moved in this example. We have just observed the effect of circumstances and of physical temperature. Strictly speaking, these have not produced the orange; the seeds were given, and these alone contained the vital force. The circumstances described, however, were necessary in order that the plant might flourish and be propagated; had these failed, the plant likewise would have failed.

Accordingly, let the temperature be different, and the species of plant will be different. Suppose conditions entirely opposite to those just mentioned; take the summit of a mountain swept by violent winds, with a thin scanty soil, a cold climate, a short summer, and snow during the winter; not only will the orange not thrive here, but the greater part of other trees will perish. Of all the seeds scattered haphazard by the wind only one will survive, and you will see but one species to endure and be propagated, the only one adapted to these severe conditions; the fir and the pine will cover the lonely crags, the abrupt precipices, and long, rocky ridges, with their stiff colonnades of tall trunks and vast mantles of sombre green, and there, as in the Vosges, in Scotland and in Norway, you may travel league after league, under silent arches, on a carpet of crisp leaves, among gnarled roots obstinately clinging to the rocks, the domain of the patient energetic plant which alone subsists under the incessant attacks of gales, and the hoar-frosts of long winters.

We may accordingly regard temperature and physical circumstances as *making a choice* amongst various species of trees, all owing a certain species to subsist and propagate, to the exclusion, more or less complete, of all others. Physical temperature acts by elimination and suppression, in other words, by *natural selection.* Such is the great law by which we now explain the origin and structure of diverse existing organisms—a law as applicable to moral as to physical conditions, to history as well as to botany and zoology, to genius and to character, as well as to plant and to animal.

In short, there is a *moral* temperature, consisting of the general state of minds and manners, which acts in the same way as the other. Properly speaking, this temperature does not produce artists; talent and genius are gifts like seeds; what I mean to say is, that the same country at different epochs probably contains about the same number of men of talent, and of men of mediocrity. We know, in fact, through statistics, that in two successive generations nearly the same number of men are found of the requisite stature for the conscription and the same number of men too small for soldiers. In all probability, it is with minds as with bodies. Nature is a sower of men, and putting her hand constantly in the same sack, distributes nearly the same quantity, the same quality, the same proportion of seed. But in these handfuls of seed which she scatters as she strides over time and space, not all germinate. A certain moral temperature is necessary to develop certain talents; if this is wanting, these prove abortive. Consequently, as the temperature changes, so will the species of talent change; if it becomes reversed, talent will become reversed, and, in general, we may conceive moral temperature as *making a selection* among different species of talent, allowing only this or that species to develope, to the exclusion more or less complete of others. It is through some such mechanism that you see developed in schools at certain times and in certain countries the sentiment of the ideal, that of the real, that of drawing and that of color. There is a prevailing tendency which constitutes the spirit of the age. Talent seeking to force an outlet in another direction, finds it closed; and the force of the public mind and surrounding habits repress and lead it astray, by imposing on it a fixed growth.

III.

The foregoing comparison may serve you as a general indication; let us now enter into details, and study the action of the moral temperature on works of art.

For the sake of greater clearness we will take a very simple case, that of a certain mental condition, in which melancholy predominates. This supposition is not arbitrary, for such a condition has frequently occurred in the life of humanity: five or six centuries of decadence, depopulation, foreign invasion, famine, pests, and aggravated misery, are amply sufficient to produce it. Asia experienced such a state of things in the sixth century before Christ, and Europe in the period of the first ten centuries of our own era. In times like these men lose both courage and hope, and regard life as a burden.

Let as contemplate the effect of such a mental condition, together with the circumstances which engender it, on the artists of an epoch like this. We admit that nearly the same number of melancholy and joyous temperaments, as well as a mixture of both, are met in this as at other times; how and in what sense does the prevailing situation effect their transformation?

It must be borne in mind that the misfortunes that afflict the public also afflict the artist; he is one of the flock, and he suffers as the rest suffer. For example, if invasions of barbarians occur, and pests, famines, and calamities of all sorts prolonged for centuries and spread over the entire country; not only one, but countless miracles, would be necessary to save him harmless in the general inundation. On the contrary, it is probable, and even certain, that he will have his share of public misfortune; that he will be ruined, beaten, wounded, and led into captivity like others; that his wife, children, relatives and friends will share the common fate, and that he will suffer and be subject to fears on their account, as well as on his own. During this long-continued flood of personal misery he will, if he is gay, become less gay, and, if melancholy, still more melancholy. This is the first effect of his social medium.

On the other hand, if the artist is raised among melancholy companions, the ideas he receives in infancy, with those acquired afterwards, are melancholy. The dominant religion, accommodating itself to the lugubrious order of things, teaches him that the earth is a place of exile, the world a prison-house, life an evil, and that all that concerns him is to deserve to get out of it. Philosophy, forming its morality according to the lamentable spectacle of man's degeneracy, proves to him that it would have been better for him not to have been born Ordinary conversation teems with only mournful events, the invasion of a province, the destruction of some monument, the oppression of the weak, and civil wars among the strong. Daily observation reveals to him only images of discouragement and grief, beggars, and cases of starvation, a bridge left to decay, abandoned, crumbling houses, fields going to waste, and the black walls of dwellings ravaged by fire. All these impressions sink deep in his mind from the first year of his life to the last, incessantly aggravating whatever melancholy sentiment arises out of his own misfortunes.

They aggravate him so much the more proportionately to the intensity of his artistic feeling. What makes him an artist is the practice of imitating the essential character of things, the salient points of objects; other men only see portions, while he sees the whole and the spirit of them. And as in this case the salient characteristic is melancholy, he accordingly perceives nothing else. Moreover, through this excess of imagination and this instinct of exaggeration peculiar to artists, he amplifies and expands it to the utmost; he becomes impregnated with it, and charges his work with it, so that he commonly sees and paints things in much darker colors than would be employed by his contemporaries.

It must be added also that he finds them of great assistance to him in his work. You know that a man who paints or writes remains not alone face to face with his canvas or his writing-desk. On the contrary, he goes out and talks to people and looks about him; he listens to the hints of his friends or rivals, and seeks suggestions in books and from surrounding works of art. An idea resembles a seed: if the seed requires, in order to germinate, develope and bloom, the nourishment which water, air, sun and soil afford it, the idea, in order to complete and shape itself into form, requires to be supplemented and aided by other minds. Accordingly, in these epochs of melancholy, what sort of suggestions are other minds capable of furnishing? Only melancholy ones, for only on this side do men labor. As their experience provides them only with painful sensations and sentiments, they can only note the shades of difference, and record discoveries made on the path of suffering: the heart is the only field of observation, and if this is filled with sorrow, sorrow is all that men contemplate. They are, therefore, conscious only of grief, dejection, chagrin and despair. If the artist demands instruction of them this is all the return they can make. To seek in them any idea or any information on the different kinds or different expressions of joy would be labor lost; they can only furnish what they possess. For this reason let him attempt to portray happiness, cheerfulness, or gayety, and he stands alone, deprived of all support, left to his own resources, and which in an isolated man amounts to nothing. His labor will likewise be stamped with mediocrity. On the other hand, when he would paint melancholy sentiments his century would come to his aid. He finds materials prepared for him by preceding schools; he finds a ready-made art, consisting of known processes and a beaten track. A church ceremony, a piece of furniture, a conversation, suggests to him a form, a color, a phrase, or a character still unknown to him; his work, to which millions of unknown co-laborers have contributed, is all the more beautiful, because, in addition to his own labor and his own genius, it embodies the labor and genius of surrounding society, and of generations that have gone before it.

There is still another reason, and the strongest of all, which draws him to melancholy subjects; it is that his work, once exposed to the public eye, finds appreciation only as it expresses melancholy ideas. Men, indeed, can only comprehend sentiments analogous to those they have themselves experienced. Other sentiments, no matter how powerfully expressed, do not affect them; the look with their eyes, but the heart is dormant and directly their eyes are averted. Imagine a man losing his fortune, country, children, health and liberty, one manacled in a dungeon for twenty years, like Pellico or Andryane, whose spirit by degrees is changed and broken, and who becomes melancholy and a mystic, and whose discouragement is incurable; such a man entertains a horror of cheerful music, and has no disposition to read Rabelais; if you place him before the merry brutes of Rubens, he will turn aside and place himself before the canvases of Rembrandt; he will enjoy only the music of Chopin and the poetry of Lamartine or Heine. The same thing happens to the public and to individuals; their taste depends on their situation; their sadness gives them a taste for melancholy works; cheerful productions are accordingly repudiated, and the artist is censured or neglected. Now an artist composes mostly in order to obtain appreciation and applause; this is his ruling passion. Hence, therefore, betides other causes, his ruling passion, added to the pressure of public opinion, leads him, pushes him, and constantly brings him back to the expression of melancholy, and barring the ways to him which would lead him to the portrayal of gayety and happiness.

Through this series of obstacles every passage would be closed for works of art manifesting joy. If an artist overcomes one obstacle, he is arrested by others. If he meets with joyous natures he will be saddened *by* their personal misfortunes. Education and current conversation fill their minds with gloomy ideas. The artists' faculties by which they detach and amplify the leading traits of objects, will find for their exercise none but melancholy ones. The experience and labor of others provide them with suggestions and are co-operative only in melancholy subjects. Finally, the earnest and decisive will of the public allows them to produce only melancholy subjects. Consequently, the class of artists and their works suitable for the expression of gayety and joyousness disappear, or end by becoming reduced to almost nothing.

Consider, now, the opposite case, that of a general condition of cheerfulness. That occurs in renaissance epochs, when order, wealth, population, comfort, prosperity, and useful and beautiful discoveries are constantly increasing. By reversing its terms the analysis we have just made is applicable word for word;

the same process of reasoning proves that the works of art of such a period will all, more or less, express a joyous character.

Consider, now, an intermediary case, that is to say, a commingling of this or that phase of joy or sadness, which is the ordinary condition of things. By a proper modification of terras, the analysis is equally pertinent; the same reasoning demonstrates that works of art express corresponding combinations, and a corresponding species of joy and melancholy.

Let us conclude, therefore, that in every simple or complex state, the social medium, that is to say, the general state of mind and manners, determines the species of works of art in suffering only those which are in harmony with it, and in suppressing other species, through a series of obstacles interposed, and a series of attacks renewed, at every step of their development.

IV.

Let us now leave supposed cases, simplified to give clearness to the exposition, and take up real ones. You will see in glancing at the most important of a historical series, a verification of the law. I will select four which are the four great cycles of European civilization—Greek and Roman antiquity, the feudal and Christian middle ages, the well-regulated aristocratic monarchies of the seventeenth century, and the industrial democracies of the present day, directed by the sciences. Each of these periods has its own art, or some department of art peculiar to it, either sculpture, architecture, the drama or music, or some determined phase of each of these great arts; in every case a distinct, singularly rich and complete vegetation, which, in its leading features, reflects the principal traits of the art and the nation. Let us, accordingly, consider turn the different soils, and we shall that all produce different flowers.

V.

About three thousand years ago there appeared on the shores and islands of the Ægean Sea a remarkably handsome, intelligent race, viewing life in quite a new way. It did not allow itself to be absorbed by a great religious conception like the Hindoos and Egyptians, nor by a great social organization like the Assyrians and Persians, nor by great industrial and commercial usages after the fashion of the Phoenicians and Carthagenians. Instead of a theocracy and a hierarchy of caste, and instead of a monarchy and a hierarchy of functionaries and of great trading and commercial establishments, the men of that race had an invention of their own called the city, which city, in sending forth branches, gave birth to others of the same description. One of these, Miletus, produced three hundred towns, and colonized the entire coast of the Black Sea. Others did the same, the Mediterranean Sea being encircled with a garland of flourishing cities, extending from Cyrene to Marseilles, along the gulfs and promontories of Spain, Italy, Greece, Asia Minor and Africa.

What was the life of this city?[1] A citizen performed but little manual labor; he was generally supported by his subjects and tributaries, and always served by slaves. The poorest man in the place had one to keep house for him. Athens counted four for each citizen; and lesser cities, like Ægina and Corinth, possessed from four to five hundred thousand. Servants, of course, abounded. The citizen, however, needed but little help. Like all the finely-built races of the south, he was abstemious, a meal consisting of three or four olives, a bit of garlic, and the head of a fish.[2] His wardrobe consisted of sandals, a small shirt, and a large mantle, like that of a shepherd. His house was a narrow, frail, ill-constructed tenement, into which robbers could penetrate by piercing the walls,[3] and which he only used for sleeping; a bed and two or three beautiful vases were the principal articles of furniture. The citizen had few wants, and he passed the day in the open air.

How did he dispose of his leisure? Serving neither king nor priest, he was, as far as he was concerned, free and sovereign in the city. He elected his own pontiffs and magistrates, and he himself, in turn, could be elected to sacerdotal and other offices; whether blacksmith or currier, he judged the most important political cases in the tribunals, and decided the gravest of affairs of state in the assemblies; his occupation consisted, substantially, of public business and war. To be a politician and a soldier was a part of his duty; other pursuits were of little importance to him; the attention of a free man, in his opinion, ought to be applied to these two employments. And he was right, for, at that time, human life was not protected as it is in ours; human societies had not acquired the stability which they now have. Most of these cities, built and scattered along the Mediterranean shores, were surrounded by barbarians eager to prey upon them; the citizen was obliged to be under arms, like the European of the present day in Japan and in New Zealand; if not, Gauls, Libyans, Samitites and Bithynians would soon have pitched their camps amid the ruins of battered walls and devastated temples. Besides all this, these cities were inimical to each other. The rights of war were atrocious; a vanquished city was often devoted to destruction; a wealthy noted man might any day see his dwelling in ashes, his property pillaged, his wife and daughters sold to recruit places of prostitution; he himself, and his sons, enslaved, would be buried in mines, or compelled by the lash to turn a mill. With such perils before him it is natural for a man to be interested in affairs of state, and be qualified for battle: he has to become a politician under penalty of death. Ambition, however, and love of glory are equal stimulants. Every city aspired to reduce or humble every other city, to acquire vassals, to conquer or to make profitable the persons of others.[4] The citizen passed his life in the public thoroughfares, discussing the best means for preserving and aggrandizing his city, canvassing its alliances, treaties, laws and constitution; now listening to orators, and again acting as one himself up to the very moment of going aboard his vessel in order to wage war in Thrace or in Egypt, against other Greeks, against the barbarians, or against the Great King.

To reach this point, they had systematized a peculiar discipline. As there were no industrial facilities in those days, the machinery of war was unknown. War was a combat between man and man; consequently, the essential thing to insure victory was not to transform soldiers into marshalled automatons, as in our day, but to render each soldier the most resistant, the strongest, and the most agile body possible; in short, a highly-tempered gladiator, capable of the utmost physical endurance.

To this end, Sparta which, about the eighth century, gave the example and the impulse to all Greece, had a very complicated and no less efficacious military system. She herself was a camp without walls, situated, like our camps in Kabyle, amidst enemies and a conquered people, wholly military, and devoted to attack and self-defence. In order to have a perfect military, it was necessary to have a splendid race; it was managed as in stock-breeding. All deformed children were deprived of life. The law, moreover, prescribed the age for marriage and selected the most suitable time and circumstances for proper breeding. An old man happening to have a young wife was obliged to give her over to a young man in order to have a good healthy offspring. A middle-aged man having a friend whose beauty and character he admired, might give him the use of his wife.[5] After having constituted the race, they shaped the individual. Young men were enrolled, drilled, and accustomed to live in common like a troop of children. They were divided into two rival bands, who inspected each other, and fought together with their feet and their fists. They slept in the open air, bathed in the cool waters of the Eurotas, went marauding, ate sparingly, fast and badly, rested on beds of rushes, drank nothing but water, and endured every inclemency of climate. Young girls exercised in the same manner, and the matured were restricted to almost the same routine. The rigor of this antique discipline was undoubtedly less, or was mitigated, in other cities; nevertheless, with these mitigations, the same road conducted to the same end. Young people passed the greater part of the day in the gymnasia, wrestling, jumping, boxing, racing, pitching quoits; fortifying and rendering supple their naked muscles. It was their aim to produce strong, robust bodies, the most beautiful and the nimblest possible, and no system of education ever succeeded better in obtaining them.[6]

These peculiar customs of the Greeks gave birth to peculiar ideas. In their eyes the ideal man was not the man of thought, or a man of delicate sensibility, but the naked man, the man of a fine stock and growth, well-proportioned, active and accomplished in all physical exercises. This mode of thinking was manifested by a variety of traits. In the first place, whilst the Carians and the Lydians around them, and their barbarian neighbors generally, were ashamed to appear naked, they stripped without embarrassment in order to wrestle and run races.[7] The young girls of Sparta were in the habit of exercising almost naked. You will perceive that gymnastic exercises had suppressed, or at least transformed, modesty. In the second place, the great national festivals of the Greeks, the Olympian, Pythian, and Nemean games, consisted of a display and triumph of the naked figure. The youth of the first families resorted to these from all parts of Greece, and from the remotest Grecian colonies. They, prepared themselves for them a long time beforehand by special training and the severest labor, and there, under the eyes and applause of the whole nation, stripped of their clothing, they wrestled, boxed, pitched quoits, and raced on foot or in the chariot. Victories of this class, which we of the present day leave to a Hercules in a circus, they regarded as of the first importance. The victorious athlete in the footrace gave his name to the Olympiad; his praises were chanted by the greatest poets; Pindar, the most illustrious lyric poet of antiquity, sang only of chariot races. On returning to his native city the victorious athlete was received in triumph, and his strength and agility became the pride of the place. One of these, Milo of Crotona, who was invincible at wrestling, was chosen general, and led his fellow-citizens to battle, clad in a lion's skin and armed with a club like Hercules, to whom he was compared. It is related that a certain Diagoras saw his two sons crowned on the same day, and was carried around by them in triumph before the assembled multitude. Deeming a like happiness too great for one mortal, the people cried out to him. "Die, Diagoras, for thou canst not now become a god!" Diagoras, suffocated with emotion, did indeed expire in the arms of his children. In his eyes, as in the eyes of all Greece, to see his sons possessing the most vigorous fists and the nimblest legs was the height of terrestrial bliss. Whether this be truth or legend, such a judgment proves the excessive degree of admiration entertained by the Greeks for the perfection of the human form.

On this account they were not afraid to expose it before the gods on solemn occasions. They had a formal system of attitudes and actions, called *orchestrique,* which regulated and taught them beautiful postures of the sacred dances. After the battle of Salamis the tragic poet Sophocles, then fifteen years old, and celebrated for his beauty, stripped himself of his clothing in order to dance and chant the pæan before the trophy. One hundred years later, Alexander, on passing through Asia Minor to contend with Darius, cast aside his garments, along with his companions, for the purpose of honoring the tomb of Achilles with races. But the Greeks went still further; they considered the perfection of the human form as attesting divinity. In a town in Sicily a young man of extraordinary beauty was worshipped, and after death, altars were erected in his honor.[8] In Homer, which is the Grecian Bible, you will find everywhere that the gods had a human body which the flesh-lance could pierce, flowing red blood, instincts, passions and pleasures similar in every respect to our own, and to such an extent that heroes become the lovers of goddesses, and gods beget children of mortal mothers. Between Olympus and the earth there is no abyss; they descend from, and we ascend to, it; if they surpass us, it is because they are exempt from death, because their wounds heal quicker, and they are stronger, handsomer and happier than we. In other respects, they eat, drink and quarrel as we do, all enjoying the same senses, and employing the same corporeal functions. Greece has so well worked out its model of the beautiful human animal that it has made its idol of it, and glorifies it on earth, by making a divinity of it in heaven.

Out of this conception statuary is born, and we can mark every moment of its growth. On the one hand, an athlete, once crowned, was entitled to a statue; crowned a third time, he was awarded an iconical statue—that is to say, an effigy bearing his portrait. On the other hand, the gods being only human forms, more serene and more perfect than others, it was natural to represent them by statues. For that purpose there is no need of a forced dogma. The marble or bronze effigy is not an allegory, but an exact image; it does not give to the god muscles, bones, and a heavy covering which it has not; it represents the reclothing of flesh which covers it, and the living form which is its substance. It suffices, in order to be a truthful portrait, that it should be the most beautiful, and reproduce the immortal calm by which the god is exalted above mortals.

The statue is now blocked out—is the sculptor qualified to produce it? Dwell a moment on his preparation. Men in those days studied the body naked and in action, in the baths, in the gymnasia, in the sacred dances and at the public games; they observed and preferred such forms and such attitudes as denoted vigor, health, and activity; they labored with all their might to impress on it these forms and to shape it to these attitudes. For three or four hundred years they were thus correcting, purifying, developing their idea of physical beauty. It is not surprising that they finally discovered the ideal type of the human form. We of the present day that are familiar with it owe our knowledge of it to them. When Nicholas of Pisa and other early sculptors at the end of the Gothic period abandoned the meagre, bony, and ugly forms of hieratic tradition, it was because they took an example from Greek bas-reliefs, preserved or exhumed; and if to-day, forgetting our distorted and defective bodies, as plebeians or thinkers, we wish to find again some type of the perfect form, it is in these statues, monuments of a noble, unoccupied, gymnastic life, that we must seek our instruction.

Not only the form of it is perfect, but again, which is unique, it suffices for the thought of the artist. The Greeks, having assigned to the body a dignity of its own, were not tempted, like the moderns, to subordinate it to the head. A chest breathing healthily, a trunk solidly resting on the thighs, a nervous supple leg impelling the body forward with ease; they did not occupy themselves solely with the breadth of a thoughtful forehead, with the frown of an irritated brow, or the turn of a sarcastic lip. They could limit themselves to the conditions of perfect statuary, which leaves the eye without an iris, and the head without expression; which prefers quiet personages, or those occupied by insignificant action; which commonly employs only a uniform tint, either of marble or cf bronze; which leaves the picturesque to painting, and abandons dramatic interest to literature; which, confined to, but ennobled by, the nature of its materials and its limited domain, avoids the representation of details, of physiognomy, of the casualties of human agitation, in order to detach the pure and abstract form, and thus illuminate the sanctuaries with motionless, peaceful, august effigies in which human nature recognized its heroes and its gods.

Statuary, accordingly, is the central art of Greece; other arts are related to it, accompany it, or imitate it. No other art has so well expressed the national life; no other was so cultivated or so popular. In the hundred small temples around Delphi, in which the treasures of the cities were kept, "a whole world of marble, gold, silver, brass, and bronze, twenty different bronzes, and of all tints, thousands of glorified dead in irregular groups, seated and standing, radiated the veritable subjects of the god of light."[9] When Rome, at a later day, despoiled the Greek world of its treasures, this vast city possessed a population of statues almost equal to that of its living inhabitants. At the present time, after so many centuries and such devastation, it is estimated that more than sixty thousand statues have been discovered at Rome and in its surrounding Campagna. A like harvest of sculpture has never been seen, such a prodigious abundance of flowers,—a display of flowers so perfect, a growth so natural, so continuous and varied. You have just seen the cause of it, in digging up the earth layer by layer, and in observing that all the foundations of the human soil, institutions, manners, ideas, have contributed to sustain it.

[1] Grote, *History of Greece*—Boeckh, *Political Economy of the Athenians*—Wullon, *Slavery in Antiquity.*

[2] The Frogs of Aristophanes; the Cock of Lucian.

[3] Their proper name was wall-piercers.

[4] Thucydides, Book I. See the divers expeditions of the Athenians between the peace of Cimon and the Peloponnesian war.

[5] Xenophon. The Lacedemonian Republic, *passim.*

[6] The Dialogues of Plato. The Clouds of Aristophanes.

[7] The Lacedemonians adopted this custom about the 14th Olympiad.—Plato.

[8] Herodotus.

[9] Michelet.

VI.

This military organization common to all the cities of antiquity at length had its effect,—a sad effect. War being the natural condition of things, the weak were over-powered by the strong, and, more than once, one might have seen formed states of considerable magnitude under the control or tyranny of a victorious or dominant city. Finally one arose, Rome, which, possessing greater energy, patience, and skill, more capable of subordination and command, of consecutive views and practical calculations, attained, after seven hundred years of effort, in incorporating under her dominion the entire basin of the Mediterranean and many great outlying countries. To gain this point she submitted to military discipline, and, like a fruit springing from its germ, a military despotism was the issue. Thus was the Empire formed. Towards the first century of our era, the world, organized under a regular monarchy, seemed at last to have attained to order and tranquillity. It issued only in a decline. In the horrible destruction of conquest cities perished by hundreds and men by millions. During an entire century the conquerors themselves massacred each other, and the civilized world having lost its free men, lost the half of its inhabitants.[1] Citizens, converted into subjects, and no longer pursuing noble ends, abandoned themselves to indolence and luxury, refused to marry and to have children. Machinery being unknown, and the hand the only instrument of labor, the slaves, whose lot it was to provide for the pleasures, pomp, and refinements of society, disappeared under a burden too heavy for them to bear. At the expiration of four hundred years the enervated, depopulated empire had not sufficient men or energy to repel the barbarians. The barbarous wave entered, sweeping away the dykes; after the first, a second, then a third, and so on for a period of five hundred years. The evils they inflicted cannot be described: people exterminated, monuments destroyed, fields devastated, and cities burnt; industry, the fine arts, and the sciences mutilated, degraded, forgotten; fear, ignorance, and brutality spread everywhere and established. They were complete savages, similar to the Hurons and Iroquois suddenly encamped in the midst of a cultivated and thinking world like ours. Imagine a herd of wild bulls let loose amid the furniture and decorations of a palace, and after this another herd, so that the ruins left by the first perished under the hoofs of the second, and, scarcely installed in disorder, each troop of brutes had to arouse itself in order to battle with its horns a bellowing, insatiable troop of invaders. When at last, in the tenth century, the last horde had made its lair and glutted itself, men seemed to be in no better condition. The barbarian chiefs becoming feudal barons, fought amongst themselves, pillaging peasants and burning their crops, robbing the merchants, and wantonly robbing and maltreating their miserable serfs. The land remained waste, and provisions became scarce. In the eleventh century forty out of seventy years were years of famine. A monk, Raoul Glaber, relates that it got to be common to eat human flesh; a butcher was burnt alive for exposing it for sale in his stall. Add to this universal poverty and filth, and a total neglect of the simplest of hygienic principles, and you can well understand how leprosy, pests, and epidemics, becoming acclimated, raged as if upon their native soil. People degenerated to the condition of the anthropophāgi of New Zealand, to the ignoble brutality of the Papuans and Caledonians, to the lowest depths of the human cesspool, seeing that reminiscences of the past trenched on the misery of the present, and since some thinking heads, still reading the ancient language felt in a confused way the immensity of the fall, the whole depth of the abyss into which the human species had been engulphed for a thousand years.

You may divine the sentiments which such a condition of things, so extreme and so lasting, implanted in people's breasts. At first there was weakness, disgust of life, and the deepest melancholy; "the world," said a writer of that day, "is nothing but an abyss of vice and immodesty." Life seemed a foretaste of hell. Many withdrew from it, and not alone the poor, the feeble, and women, but sovereign lords, and even kings; such as possessed delicate and noble natures preferred the tranquillity and monotony of the cloister. On the approach of the year one thousand a general belief in the extinction of the world prevailed, and many, seized with fright, made over their property to churches and convents. On the other hand, and coupled with this terror and despondency, there arose an extraordinary degree of nervous exaltation. When men are very miserable they become excitable, like invalids and prisoners; their sensibility increases, and acquires a feminine delicacy; their heart is filled with caprices, agitations and despondency, excesses and effusions from which they are free in a healthy state. They depart from moderate sentiments which alone can maintain continuous masculine action. They indulge in re very, burst into tears, sink down on their knees, become incapable of providing for themselves, imagine infinite sweet and tender transports, yearning to diffuse the excessive refinements and enthusiasm of their overwrought intemperate imaginations; in short, they are prone to love. Hence, we see them developed with an enormous exaggeration, a passion unknown to the stern and virile souls of antiquity, namely, the chivalric mystic love of the middle ages. The calm rational love of wedlock was subordinated to the ecstatic and unruly love encountered outside of wedlock. Its subtleties were carefully defined and embodied in the maxims of tribunals presided over by ladies. It was decreed there that "love could not exist between spouses," and that "love could refuse nothing to love.[2] Woman was no longer considered as flesh and blood like man, but was converted into a divinity; man was only too well compensated in the privilege of adoring: and serving her. Human love was regarded as a celestial sentiment leading to divine love and confounded with it. Poets transformed their mistresses into supernatural virtue, and implored them to guide them through the empyrean to the tabernacle of God. You can easily appreciate the hold the Christian faith derived from such sentiments. Disgust for the world, a tendency to ecstacy, habitual despair and infinite craving for tender sympathy, naturally impelled men to a doctrine representing the earth as a vale of tears, the present life a period of trial, rapturous union with the Divinity as supreme happiness, and the love of God as the first of duties. Morbid or trembling sensibility found its support in the infinitude of terror and of hope, in pictures of flaming pits and eternal perdition, and in conceptions of a radiant paradise and of ineffable bliss. Thus supported, Christianity ruled all souls, inspired art, and gave employment to artists. "Society," says a contemporary, "divested itself of its old rags in order to clothe its churches in robes of whiteness." Gothic architecture accordingly made its appearance.

Let us observe the growth of the new Gothic edifice. In opposition to the religions of antiquity, which were all local, belonging to castes or to families, Christianity is a universal religion which appeals to the multitude, and summons all men to salvation. It was necessary accordingly for this new edifice to be very large and capable of containing the entire population of any one city or district—the women, the children, the serfs, the artisans, and the poor as well as the nobles and sovereigns. The small *cella* which contains the statue of the Greek god, and the portico where the procession of free citizens was displayed, were not sufficient for this immense crowd. An enormous vault was required, lofty naves multiplied and crossed by others, and measureless arches and colossal columns; generations of workmen flocked in crowds for centuries to labor here for the salvation of their souls, displacing mountains before the monument could be completed.

The men who enter here have sorrowing souls, and the ideas they come in quest of are mournful. They meditate on this miserable life, so troubled and confined by such an abyss, on hell and its punishments, endless, measureless and unintermittent, on the sufferings and passion of Christ crucified, and those of persecuted and tortured saints and martyrs. Listening to such religious teaching, and under the burden of their own fears, they could ill accommodate themselves to the simple beauty and joyous effect of pure light; the clear and healthy light of day is accordingly excluded; the interior of the edifice remains subject to cold and lugubrious shadow; light only comes in transformed by stained glass into purple and crimson tints, into the splendors of topaz and amethyst, into the mystic gleams of precious stones, into strange illuminations, seeming to afford glimpses of paradise.

Delicate over-excited imaginations like these are not content with simple architectural forms. And first, form in itself is not sufficient to interest them. It must be a symbol of and designate some august mystery. The edifice with its transverse naves represents the cross on which Christ died; its circular window with its brilliant petals figures the rose of eternity, the leaves of which are redeemed souls; all the dimensions of its parts correspond to sacred numbers. Again, these forms in their richness, strangeness, boldness, delicacy and immensity, harmonize with the intemperance and curiosity of a morbid fancy. Vivid sensations—manifold, changing, bizarre and extreme—are necessary to such souls. They reject the column, the horizontal and transverse beams, the round arch, in short, the solid construction, balanced proportions, and beautiful simplicity of antique architecture; they do not sympathize with those noble creations that seem to have been born without pain and to last without effort, which attain to beauty the same time as to life, and the finished excellence of which needs neither addition nor ornament.

They adopt for type, not the plain half-circle of the arcade, or the simple angle formed by the column and the architrave, but the complicated union of two curves intersected by each other, forming the ogive. They aspire to the gigantic, covering square acres of ground with piles of stone, binding pillars together in monstrous columns, suspending galleries in the air, elevating arches to the skies, and stage upon stage of belfry until their spires are lost in the clouds. They exaggerate the delicacy of forms; they surround doors with series of statuettes, and festoon the sides with trefoils, gables and gargoyles; they interlace the tortuous tracery of mullions with the motley hues of stained glass; the choir seems to be embroidered with lace, while tombs, altars, stalls and towers are covered with mazes of slender columns and fringes of leaves and statues. It seems as if they wished to attain at once infinite grandeur and infinite littleness, seeking to overwhelm the mind on either side, on the one hand with the vastness of a mass, and on the other with a prodigious quantity of details. Their object was evidently to produce an extraordinary sensation; they aimed to dazzle and bewilder.

Proportionately, therefore, to the development of this style of architecture, it becomes more and more paradoxical. In the fourteenth and fifteenth centuries, the age of the flamboyant Gothic of Strasburg, Milan, York, Nuremburg, and the Church of Brou, solidity seems to have been wholly abandoned for ornament. At one time it bristles with a profusion of multiplied and superposed pinnacles; at another its exterior is draped with a lacework of mouldings. Walls are hollowed out, and almost wholly absorbed by windows; they lack strength, and without the buttresses raised against them the structure would fall; ever disintegrating, it is necessary to establish colonies of masons about them constantly to repair their constant decay. This embroidered stonework, more and more frail as it ascends the spire, cannot sustain itself; it has to be fastened to a skeleton of iron, and as iron rusts, the blacksmith is summoned to contribute his share towards propping up this unstable, delusive magnificence. In the interior the decoration is so exuberant and complex, the groinings so richly display their thorny and tangled vegetation, and the stalls, pulpit, and railings, swarm with such intricate, tortuous, fantastic arabesques, that the church no longer seems to be a sacred monument, but a rare example of the jewellers art. It is a vast structure of variegated glass, a gigantic piece of filigree work, a festive decoration as elaborated as that of a queen or a bride; it is the adornment of a nervous, over-excited woman, similar to the extravagant costumes of the day, whose delicate and morbid poesy denotes by its excess the singular sentiments, the feverish, violent, and impotent aspiration peculiar to an age of knights and monks.

For this architecture, which has lasted four centuries, is not confined to one country or to one description of edifice; it is spread over all Europe, from Scotland to Sicily, and is employed in all civil and religious and public and private monuments. Not only do cathedrals and chapels bear its imprint, but fortresses, palaces, costumes, dwellings, furniture, and equipments. Its universality, accordingly, expresses and attests the great moral crisis, at once morbid and sublime, which, during the whole of the middle ages, exalted, and at the same time disordered, the human intellect.

[1] *Rome, thirty years B. C,* by Victor Durny.

[2] Andre le Chapelain.

VII

Human institutions, like living bodies, are made and unmade by their own forces; and their health passes away or their cure is effected by the sole effect of their nature and their situation. Among these feudal chiefs who ruled and plundered men in the middle-ages one was found in each country, stronger, more politic, and better placed than others, who constituted himself conservator of public order; sustained by public sentiment, he by degrees weakened and subdued, subordinated and rallied the others, and, organizing a systematic obedient administration, became under the name of king the head of the nation. Towards the fifteenth century, the barons, formerly his equals, were only his officers, and towards the seventeenth century they were simply his courtiers.

Note the significance of this term. A courtier is a member of the king's court; that is to say, a person charged with some function or domestic duty in the palace—either chamberlain, equerry, or gentleman of the antechamber—receiving a salary, and addressing his master with all the deference and ceremonial obsequiousness proper to such an employment. But this person is not a valet, as in oriental monarchies, for his ancestor, the grandfather of his grandfather, was the equal, the companion, the peer of the king; and on this account he himself belongs to a privileged class, that of noblemen. He does not serve his prince solely through personal interest; his devotion to him is a point of honor. The prince in his turn never neglects to treat him with consideration. Louis XIV. threw his cane out of the window in order not to be tempted to strike Lauzun, who had offended him. The courtier is honored by his master, and regarded as one of his society. He lives in familiarity with him, dances at his balls, dines at his table, rides in the same carriage, sits in the same chairs, and frequents the same *salon*. From such a basis court life arose; first in Italy and Spain, subsequently in France, and afterwards in England, in Germany, and in the north of Europe. France was its centre, and Louis XIV. gave to it its principal *éclat*.

Let us study the effect of this new state of things on minds and characters. The kings *salon* is the first in the country, and is frequented by the most select society; the most admired personage, therefore, the accomplished man whom everybody accepts for a model, is the nobleman enjoying familiarity with his sovereign. This nobleman entertains generous sentiments; he believes himself of a superior race, and he says to himself, *noblesse oblige.* He is more sensitive than other men on the point of honor, and freely risks his life at the slightest insult. Under Louis XIII. four thousand noblemen were killed in duels. Contempt of danger, in the eyes of this nobleman, is the first obligation of a soul nobly born. The dandy, the worldling, so choice of his ribbons, so careful of his perruque, is ready to encamp in Flanders mud, and expose himself to bullets for hours together at Neerwinden. When Luxembourg announces that he is about to give battle, Versailles is deserted; all these young perfumed gallants hasten off to the army as if they were going to a ball. Finally, and through a remnant of the spirit of ancient feudalism, our nobleman regards the monarch as his natural legitimate chief: he knows he is bound to him, as the vassal formerly was to his suzerain, and at need will give him his blood, his property, and his life. Under Louis XYI. noblemen voluntarily placed themselves at the king's disposal, and on the 10th of August many were slain in his behalf.

But they are nevertheless courtiers, that is to say, men of the world, and in this respect perfectly polite. The King himself sets them an example. Louis XIV. even doffed his hat to a chambermaid, and the Memoirs of St. Simon mention a duke who saluted so frequently that he was obliged to cross the courts of Versailles bareheaded. The courtier, for the same reason, is accomplished in all that appertains to good breed-ins; language never fails him in difficult circumstances; he is a diplomat, master of himself, an adept in the art of disguising, concealing, flattering and managing others, never giving offence, and often pleasing. All these qualifications and these sentiments proceed from an aristocratic spirit refined by the usages of society; they attain to perfection in this court and in this century. Anybody of the present time disposed to admire the choice flowers of this lost and delicate species need not look for them in our equalized, rude and mixed society, but must turn to the elegant, formal, monumental parterres in which they formerly flourished.

You can imagine that people so constituted must have chosen pleasures appropriate to their character. Their taste, indeed, like their persons, was noble; for they were not only noble by birth, but also through their sentiments; and correct because they were educated to practise and respect what was becoming to them. It was this taste which, in the seventeenth century, fashioned all their works of art—the serious, elevated, severe productions of Poussin and Lesueur, the grave, pompous, elaborate architecture of Mansart and Perrault, and the stately symmetrical gardens of LeNotre. You will find its traces in the furniture, costumes, house decoration, and carriages of the engravings and paintings of Perelle, Sebastian Leclerc, Eigaud, Nanteuil, and many others. Versailles, with its groups of well-bred gods, its symmetrical alleys, its my theological water-works, its large artificial basins, its trimmed and pruned trees modelled into architectural designs, is a masterpiece in this direction; all its edifices and parterres, everything belonging to it, was constructed for men solicitous about their dignity, and strict observers of the recognized standard of social propriety. But the imprint is still more visible in the literature of the epoch. Never in France or in Europe has the art of fine writing been carried to such perfection. The greatest of French authors, as you are aware, belong to this epoch—Bossuet, Pascal, La Fontaine, Molière, Corneille, Racine, La Rochefoucauld, Madame de Sévigné, Boileau, La Bruyère, Bourdalone, and others. Great men not only wrote well, but almost everybody; Courier asserted that a chambermaid of those days knew more about style than a modern academy. In fact, a good style at that time pervaded the air, people unconsciously inhaling it; it prevailed in correspondence and in conversation; the court taught it; it entered into the ways of people of the world. The man who aimed to be polished and correct in deportment, got to be so likewise in the attributes of language and of style. Among so many branches of literature there is one, tragedy, which reached a singular degree of perfection, and which more than all the rest furnishes at that time the most striking example of the concordance which links together man and his works, manners and the arts.

The general features of this tragedy first claim attention; they are all calculated to please noblemen and members of the court. The poet does not fail in the blandishment, of truth, which by its nature is often crude; he allows no murders on the stage; he disguises brutality and repudiates violence, such as blows, butcheries, yells, and groans, everything that might offend the senses of a spectator accustomed to moderation and the elegancies of the *salon*. For the same reason he excludes disorder, never abandoning himself to the caprices of fancy and imagination like Shakespeare; his plan is regular, he admits no unforeseen incidents, no romantic poesy. He elaborates his scenes, explains entrances, graduates the interest of his piece, prepares the way for sudden turns of fortune, and skilfully anticipates and directs dénouements. Finally, he diffuses throughout the dialogue, like a uniform brilliant varnish, a studied versification composed of the choicest terms and the most harmonious rhymes. If we seek the costume of this drama in the engravings of the time we find heroes and princesses appearing in furbelows, embroideries, bootees, swords and plumes—a dress, in short, Greek in name, but French in taste and fashion; such as the king, the dauphin, and the princesses paraded in, to the music of violins, at the court performances of ballets.

Note, moreover, that all his personages are courtiers, kings and queens, princes and princesses of royal blood, ambassadors, ministers, officers of the guard, *menins,*[1] dependants and confidants. The associates of princes are not here, as in ancient Greek tragedy, slaves of the palace and nurses born under their master's roof, but ladies-in-waiting, equerries, and gentlemen of the antechamber, charged with certain duties in the royal household; we readily detect this in their conversational ability, in their skill in flattery, in their perfect education, in their exquisite deportment, and in their monarchical sentiments as subjects and vassals. Their masters, like themselves, are French noblemen of the seventeenth century, proud and courteous, heroic in Corneille and noble in Racine; they are gallants with the ladies, faithful to their name and race, capable of sacrificing their dearest interests and strongest affections to their honor, and incapable of uttering a word or an act which the most rigid courtesy would not authorize. Iphigenia, in Racine, delivered up by her father to her executioners, does not regret life, weeping like a girl, as in Euripides, but thinks it her duty to obey her father and her king without a murmur, and to die without shedding a tear, because she is a princess. Achilles, who in Homer stamps, still unappeased, on the body of the dying Hector, feeling like a lion or wolf, as if he would "eat the raw flesh" of his vanquished antagonist, is, in Racine, a Prince of Condé, at once brilliant and seductive, passionate concerning honor, devoted to the fair, impetuous, it is true, and irritable, but with the reserved vivacity of a young officer who, even when most excited, maintains good breeding and never stoops to brutality. All these characters are models of polite address, and show a knowledge of the world never at fault. Head, in Racine, the first dialogue of *Oreste* and *Pyrrhus,* and the whole of the part of *Acomat* and of *Ulysse;* nowhere is greater tact or oratorical dexterity apparent; nowhere more ingenious compliments and flatteries, exordiums so well poised, such a quick revelation, such an ingenious adjustment, such a delicate insinuation of appropriate motives. The wildest and most impetuous lovers—*Hippolyte, Britannicus, Pyrrhus, Oreste,* and *Xipharès*—are accomplished cavaliers who turn a madrigal and bow with the utmost deference. However violent their passions may be, *Hermione, Andromaqne, Boxane,* and *Bérénice,* preserve the tone of the best society. *Mithridate, Phèdre,* and *Athalie,* when expiring, express themselves in correct periods, for a prince has to be a prince to the last, and die in due form. This drama might be called a perfect picture of the fashionable world. Like Gothic architecture, it represents a positive complete side of the human mind, and this is why, like that, it has become so universal. It has been imported into, or imitated by, along with its accompanying taste, literature, and manners, every court of Europe—in England, after the restoration of the Stuarts; in Spain, on the advent of the Bourbons; and in Italy, Germany, and Russia, in the eighteenth century. We are warranted in saying that at this epoch France was the educator of Europe; she was the source from which was derived all that was elegant and agreeable, whatever was proper in style, delicate in ideas, and perfect in the art of social intercourse. If a savage Muscovite, a dull German, a stolid Englishman, or any other uncivilized or half-civilized man of the North quit his brandy, pipe, and furs, his feudal or hunting or rural life, it was to French *salons* and to French books he betook himself, in order to acquire the arts of politeness, urbanity, and conversation.

[1] Foster-brother, school-companion, or other intimate of this class.

VIII.

This brilliant society did not last; it was its own development which caused its dissolution. The government being absolute, ended in becoming negligent and tyrannical; and, besides this, the king bestowed the best offices and the greatest favor only on such of the nobles of his court as enjoyed his intimacy. This appeared unjust to the *bourgeoisie* and to the people, who, having greatly increased in numbers, wealth and intelligence, felt their power augment in proportion to the growth of their discontent. The French Revolution was accordingly their work; and after ten years of trial they established a system of democracy and equality, in which, according to a fixed order of promotion, all civil employments were ordinarily accessible to everybody. The wars of the empire and the contagion of example gradually spread this system beyond the frontiers of France, and whatever may be local differences and temporary delays, it is now evident that the tendency of the whole of Europe is to imitate it. The new construction of society, coupled with the invention of industrial machinery, and the great abatement of rudeness in manners and customs, has changed the condition as well as the character of man. Henceforth, man is exempt from arbitrary measures, and is protected by a good police. However lowly born, all careers are open to him; an enormous increase of useful articles, places within reach of the poorest, conveniences and pleasures of which, two centuries ago, the rich were entirely ignorant. Again, the rigor of authority is mitigated, both in society and in the family; a father is now the companion of his children, and the citizen has become the equal of the noble. Human life, in short, displays a lesser degree of misery, and a lighter degree of oppression.

But, as a counterpart of this, Ave see ambition and cupidity spreading their wings. Accustomed to comfort and luxuries, and obtaining here and there glimpses of happiness, man begins to regard happiness and comfort as his due. The more he obtains, the more exacting he becomes, and the more his pretensions exceed his acquisitions. The practical sciences also having made great progress, and instruction being diffused, liberated thought abandons itself to all daring enterprises; hence it happens that men, relinquishing the traditions which formerly regulated their beliefs, deem themselves capable, through intellect alone, of attaining to the highest truths. Questions of every kind are mooted, moral, political and religious; men seek knowledge by groping their way in every direction. For fifty years past we behold this strange conflict of systems and sects, each tendering us new creeds and perfect theories of happiness.

Such a state of things has a wonderful effect on minds and ideas. The representative man, that is to say, the character who occupies the stage, and to whom the spectators award the most interest and sympathy, is the melancholy, ambitious dreamer—René, Faust, Werther and Manfred—a yearning heart, restless, wandering and incurably miserable. And he is miserable for two reasons. In the first place he is over-sensitive, too easily affected by the lesser evils of life; he has too great a craving for delicate and blissful sensations; he is too much accustomed to comfort; he has not had the semi-feudal and semi-rustic education of our ancestors; he has not been roughly handled by his father, whipped at college, obliged to maintain respectful silence in the presence of great personages, and had his mental growth retarded by domestic discipline; he has not been compelled, as in ancient times, to use his own arm and sword to protect himself, to travel on horseback, and to sleep in disagreeable lodgings. In the soft atmosphere of modern comfort and of sedentary habits, he has become delicate, nervous, excitable, and less capable of accommodating himself to the course of life which always exacts effort and imposes trouble.

On the other hand, he is skeptical. Society and religion both being disturbed—in the midst of a pêle-mêle of doctrines and an irruption of new theories—his precocious judgment, too rapidly instructed, and too soon unbridled, precipitates him early and blindly off the beaten track made smooth for his fathers by habit, and which they have trodden, led on by tradition and governed by authority. All the barriers which served as guides to minds having fallen, he rushes forward into the vast, confusing field which is opened out before his eyes; impelled by almost superhuman ambition and curiosity he darts off in the pursuit of absolute truth and infinite happiness. Neither love, glory, knowledge nor power, as we find these in this world, can satisfy him; the intemperance of his desires, irritated by the incompleteness of his conquests and by the nothingness of his enjoyments, leaves him prostrate amid the ruins of his own nature, without his jaded, enfeebled, impotent imagination being able to represent to him the *beyond* which he covets, and the unknown *what* which he has not. This evil has been styled the great malady of the age. Forty years ago it was in full force, and under the apparent frigidity or gloomy impassibility of the positive mind of the present day it still subsists.

I have not the time to show you the innumerable effects of a like state of mind on works of art. You may trace them in the great development of the lyrical, sentimental and philosophical poetry of France, Germany and England; again, in the corruption and enrichment of language and in the invention of new classes and of new characters in literature; in the style and sentiments of all the great modern writers, from Chateaubriand to Balzac, from Goethe to Heine, from Cowper to Byron, and from Alfieri to Leopardi. You will find analogous symptoms in the arts of design if you observe their feverish, tortured and painfully archeological style, their aim at dramatic effect, psychological expression, and local fidelity; if you observe the confusion which has befogged the schools and injured their processes; if you pay attention to the countless gifted minds who, shaken by new emotions, have opened out new ways; if you analyze the profound sympathy for scenery which has given birth to a complete and original landscape art. But there is another art, Music, which has suddenly reached an extraordinary development. This development is one of the salient characteristics of our epoch, and the dependence of this on the modern mind, the ties by which they are connected, I shall endeavor to point out to you.

This art was born, and necessarily, in two countries where people sing naturally, Italy and Germany. It was gestating for a century and a half in Italy, from Palestrina to Pergolese, as formerly painting from Giotto to Massaccio, discovering processes and feeling its way in order to acquire its resources. At the commencement of the eighteenth century it suddenly burst forth, with Scarlatti, Marcello and Handel. This is a most remarkable epoch. Painting at this time ceased to nourish in Italy, and in the midst of political stagnation, voluptuous, effeminate customs prevailed, furnishing an assembly of sigisbés, Lindors and amorous ladies for the roulades and tender sentimental scenes of the opera. Grave, ponderous Germany, at that time the latest in acquiring self-consciousness, now succeeds in displaying the severity and grandeur of its religious sentiment, its profound knowledge, and its vague melancholy instincts in the sacred music of Sebastian Bach, anticipating the evangelical epic of Klopstock. Tn the old and in the new nation the reign and expression of *sentiment* is beginning. Between the two, half-Germanic and half-Italian, is Austria, conciliating the two spirits, producing Haydn, Gluck and Mozart. Music now becomes cosmopolite and universal on the confines of that great mental convulsion of souls styled the French Revolution, as formerly painting under the impulse of the great intellectual revival known under the name of the Renaissance. We need not be astonished at the appearance of this new art, for it corresponds to the appearance of a new genius—that of the ruling, morbid, restless, ardent character I have attempted to portray for you. It is to this spirit that Beethoven, Mendelssohn and Weber formerly addressed themselves, and to which Meyerbeer, Berlioz and Verdi are now striving to accommodate themselves.

Music is the organ of this over-refined excessive sensibility and vague boundless aspiration; it is expressly designed for this service, and no art so well performs its task. And this is so because, on the one hand, music is founded on a more or less remote imitation of a cry which is the natural, spontaneous, complete expression of passion, and which, affecting us through a corporeal stimulus, instantly arouses involuntary sympathy, so that the tremulous delicacy of every nervous being finds in it its impulse, its echo, and its ministrant. On the other hand, founded on relationships of sounds which represent no living form, and which, especially in instrumental music, seem to be the reveries of an incorporeal soul, it is better adapted than any other art to express floating thoughts, formless dreams, objectless limitless desires, the grandiose and dolorous mazes of a troubled heart which aspires to all and is attached to nothing. This is why, along with the discontent, the agitations, and the hopes of modern democracy, music has left its natal countries and diffused itself over all Europe; and why you see at the present time the most complicated symphonies attracting crowds in France, where, thus far, the national music has been reduced to the song and the melodies of the Vaudeville.

IX.

The foregoing illustrations, gentlemen, seem to me sufficient to establish the law governing the character and creation of works of art. And not only do they establish it, but they accurately define it. In the beginning of this section I stated that *the work of art is determined by an aggregate which is the general state of the mind and surrounding manners.* We may now advance another step, and note precisely in their order each link of the chain, connecting together cause and effect.

In the various illustrations we have considered, you have remarked first, a *general situation,* in other words, a certain universal condition of good or evil, one of servitude or of liberty, a state of wealth or of poverty, a particular form of society, a certain species of religious faith; in Greece, the free martial city, with its slaves; in the middle ages, feudal oppression, invasion and brigandage, and an exalted phase of Christianity; the court life of the seventeenth century; the industrial and studied democracy of the nineteenth, guided by the sciences; in short, a group of circumstances controlling man, and to which he is compelled to resign himself.

This situation developes in man corresponding needs, distinct *aptitudes* and *special sentiments*—physical activity, a tendency to revery; here rudeness, and there refinement; at one time a martial instinct, at another conversational talent, at another a love of pleasure, and a thousand other complex and varied peculiarities. In Greece we see physical perfection and a balance of faculties which no manual or cerebral excess of life deranges; in the middle ages, the intemperance of over-excited imaginations and the delicacy of feminine sensibility; in the seventeenth century, the polish and good-breeding of society and the dignity of aristocratic *salons*; and in modern times, the grandeur of unchained ambitions and the morbidity of unsatisfied yearnings.

Now, this group of sentiments, aptitudes and needs, constitutes, when concentrated in one person and powerfully displayed by him, *the representative man*, that is to say, a model character to whom his contemporaries award all their admiration and all their sympathy; there is, for instance, in Greece, the naked youth, of a fine race and accomplished in all bodily exercise; in the middle ages, the ecstatic monk and the amorous knight; in the seventeenth century, the perfect courtier; and in our days, the melancholy insatiable Faust or Werther.

Moreover, as this personage is the most captivating, the most important and the most conspicuous of all, it is he whom artists present to the public, now concentrated in an ideal personage, when their art, like painting, sculpture, the drama, the romance or the epic, is imitative; now, dispersed in its elements, as in architecture and in music, where art excites emotions without incarnating them. All their labor, therefore, may be summed up as follows: they either represent this character, or address themselves to it; the symphonies of Beethoven and the "storied windows" of cathedrals are addressed to it; and it is represented in the Niobe group of antiquity and in the Agamemnon and Achilles of Racine. *All art, therefore, depends on it,* since the whole of art is applied only to conform to, or to express it.

A general situation, provoking tendencies and special faculties; a representative man, embodying these predominant tendencies and faculties; sounds, forms, colors, or language giving this character sensuous form, or which comport with the tendencies and faculties comprising it, such are the four terms of the series; the first carries with it the second, the second the third, and the third the fourth, so that the slightest variation of either involves a corresponding variation in those that follow, and reveals a corresponding variation in those that precede it, permitting abstract reasoning in either direction in an ascending or descending scale of progression.[1] As far as I am capable of judging, this formula embraces everything. If, now, we insert between these diverse terms the accessory causes occurring to modify their effects; if, in order to explain the sentiments of an epoch, we add an examination of race to that of the social medium; if, in order to explain the works of art of any age, we consider, besides the prevailing tendencies of that age, the particular period of the art, and the particular sentiments of each artist, we shall then derive from the law not only the great revolutions and general forms of man's imagination, but, again, the differences between national schools, the incessant variations of various styles, and the original characteristics of the works of every great master. Thus followed out, such an explanation will be complete, since it furnishes at once the general traits of each school, and the distinctive traits which, in this school, characterize individuals. We are about to enter upon this study in relation to Italian art; it is a long and difficult task, and I have need of your attention in order to pursue it to the end.

[1] This law may be applied to the study of all literatures and to every art. The student may begin with the fourth term, proceeding from this to the first, strictly adhering to the order of the series.

X.

Before proceeding further, gentlemen, there is a practical and personal conclusion due to our researches, and which is applicable to the present order of things.

You have observed that each situation produces a certain state of mind followed by a corresponding class of works of art. This is why every new situation must produce a new state of mind, and consequently a new class of works; and therefore why the social medium of the present day, now in the course, of formation, ought to produce its own works like the social mediums that have gone before it. This is not a simple supposition based on the current of desire and of hope; it is the result of a law resting on the authority of experience and on the testimony of history. From the moment a law is established it is good for all time; the connections of things in the present, accompany connections of things in the past and in the future. Accordingly, it need not be said in these days that art is exhausted. It is true that certain schools no longer exist and can no longer be revived; that certain arts languish, and that the future upon which we are entering does not promise to furnish the aliment that these require. But art itself, which is the faculty of perceiving and expressing the leading character of objects, is as enduring as the civilization of which it is the best and earliest fruit. What its forms will be, and which of the five great arts will provide the A'ehicle of expression of future sentiment, we are not called upon to decide we have the right to affirm that new forms will arise, and an appropriate mould be found in which to cast them. We have only to open our eyes to see a change going on in the condition of men, and consequently in their minds, so profound, so universal, and so rapid that no other century has witnessed the like of it. The three causes that have formed the modern mind continue to operate with increasing efficacy. You are all aware that discoveries in the positive sciences are multiplying daily; that geology, organic chemistry, history, entire branches of physics and zoology, are contemporary productions; that the growth of experience is infinite, and the applications of discovery unlimited; that means of communication and transport, cultivation, trade, mechanical contrivances, all the elements of human power, are yearly spreading and concentrating beyond all expectation. None of you are ignorant that the political machine works smoother in the same sense; that communities, becoming more rational and humane, are watchful of internal order, protecting talent, aiding the feeble and the poor; in short, that everywhere, and in every way, man is cultivating his intellectual faculties and ameliorating his social condition. We cannot accordingly deny that men's habits, ideas and condition transform themselves, nor reject this consequence, that such renewal of minds and things brings along with it a renewal of art. The first period of this evolution gave rise to the glorious French school of 1830; it remains for us to witness the second—the field which is open to your ambition and your labor. On its very threshold, you have a right to augur well of your century and of yourselves; for the patient study we have just terminated shows you that to produce beautiful works, the sole condition necessary is that which the great Goethe indicated: "Fill your mind and heart, however large, with ideas and sentiments of your age, and work will follow."

THE END.

www.ingramcontent.com/pod-product-compliance
Lightning Source LLC
Chambersburg PA
CBHW021431170526
45164CB00001B/194